ANTIQUE FURNITURE

John Andrews

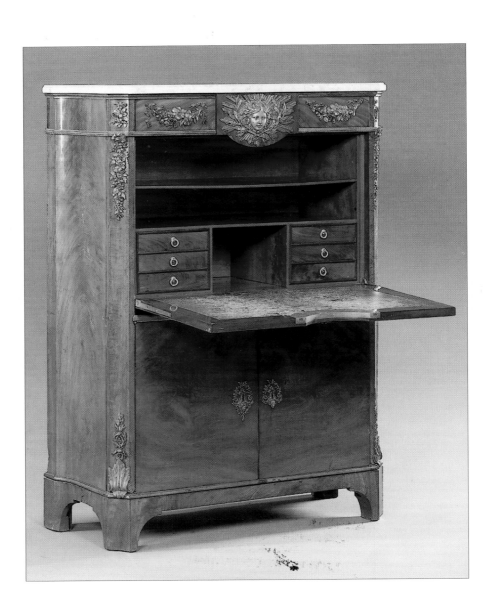

STARTING TO COLLECT SERIES

ANTIQUE FURNITURE

John Andrews

ANTIQUE COLLECTORS' CLUB

ISBN 1 85149 241 0

British Library Cataloguing-in-Publication Data
A catalogue record for this book is available from the British Library

Printed in England
by the Antique Collectors' Club Ltd., Woodbridge, Suffolk
on Consort Royal Era Satin paper
supplied by the Donside Paper Company, Aberdeen, Scotland

The Antique Collectors' Club

The Antique Collectors' Club was formed in 1966 and quickly grew to a five figure membership spread throughout the world. It publishes the only independently run monthly antiques magazine, *Antique Collecting*, which caters for those collectors who are interested in widening their knowledge of antiques, both by greater awareness of quality and by discussion of the factors which influence the price that is likely to be asked. The Antique Collectors' Club pioneered the provision of information on prices for collectors and the magazine still leads in the provision of detailed articles on a variety of subjects.

It was in response to the enormous demand for information on 'what to pay' that the price guide series was introduced in 1968 with the first edition of *The Price Guide to Antique Furniture* (completely revised 1978 and 1989), a book which broke new ground by illustrating the more common types of antique furniture, the sort that collectors could buy in shops and at auctions rather than the rare museum pieces which had previously been seen (and still to a large extent are used) to make up the limited amount of illustrations in books published by commercial publishers. Many other price guides have followed, all copiously illustrated, and greatly appreciated by collectors for the valuable information they contain, quite apart from prices. The Price Guide Series heralded the publication of many standard works of reference on art and antiques. *The Dictionary of British Art* (now in six volumes), *The Pictorial Dictionary of British 19th Century Furniture Design*, *Oak Furniture* and *Early English Clocks* were followed by many deeply researched reference works such as *The Directory of Gold and Silversmiths,* providing new information. Many of these books are now accepted as the standard work of reference on their subject.

The Antique Collectors' Club has widened its list to include books on gardens and architecture. All the Club's publications are available through bookshops world wide and a full catalogue of all these titles is available free of charge from the addresses below.

Club membership, open to all collectors, costs little. Members receive free of charge *Antique Collecting*, the Club's magazine (published ten times a year), which contains well-illustrated articles dealing with the practical aspects of collecting not normally dealt with by magazines. Prices, features of value, investment potential, fakes and forgeries are all given prominence in the magazine.

Among other facilities available to members are private buying and selling facilities and the opportunity to meet other collectors at their local antique collectors' clubs. There are over eighty in Britain and more than a dozen overseas. Members may also buy the Club's publications at special pre-publication prices.

As its motto implies, the Club is an organisation designed to help collectors get the most out of their hobby: it is informal and friendly and gives enormous enjoyment to all concerned.

For Collectors —By Collectors —About Collecting

ANTIQUE COLLECTORS' CLUB
5 Church Street, Woodbridge Suffolk IP12 1DS, UK
Tel: 01394 385501 Fax: 01394 384434
——————— or ———————
Market Street Industrial Park, Wappingers' Falls, NY 12590, USA
Tel: 914 297 0003 Fax: 914 297 0068

Acknowledgements

The author and publishers would like to thank the following for their help in the production of this book:

The Bavarian National Museum, Munich

Bonhams

Christie's

Germanisches National Museum, Nuremburg

The Marketplace Guide to Victorian Furniture Styles and Values
by Peter S. Blunden and Phil T. Dunning

The National Archaeological Museum, Athens

The National Gallery of Art, Washington D.C.

Phillips

Sotheby's

Stadtisches Museum, Wiesbaden

Contents

	PERIOD STYLE	ENGLAND	ITALY	FRANCE
1500-1630	Gothic Renaissance Classical	Tudor-Gothic Elizabethan	Cinquecento 1500-1600 High Renaissance	François 1 1515-1547 High Renaissance 1550-1610
17th century **1600-1700**	Baroque Classical	Jacobean 1603-1625 Carolean 1625-1649 Cromwellian 1649-1660 Restoration 1660-1694 William & Mary 1689-1694	Baroque 1560-1700	Louis X111 1610-1643 Louis XIV 1643-1715
Eighteenth **Century** **1700-1800**	Baroque Rococo Neo-Classical	William111 1694-1702 Queen Anne 1702-1714 George 1 1714-1727 George 11 1727-1760 George 111 1760-1811 Chippendale 1754 - Hepplewhite 1788 - Sheraton 1791 -	Baroque Rococo Venetian	Louis XIV 1643-1715 Régence 1715-1723 Louis XV 1723-1774 Louis XV1 1774-1793 Directoire 1793-1799
Nineteenth **Century** **1800-1900**	French Empire Gothic Revival Rococo 'Renaissance' Art Nouveau	Late Georgian to 1811 Regency 1811-1830 William IV 1830-1837 Victorian 1837-1901 Gothic revival 'Renaissance' Arts & Crafts Aesthetic Art Nouveau	Empire Gusto Floreale Stile Liberty	Empire 1804-1815 Restauration 1815-48 Louis XVIII 1815-24 Charles X 1824-30 Louis Philippe 1830-1848 Troubadour-Gothic Second Empire 1848-1870 Napoleon III Art Nouveau 1880-1910

GERMANY	LOW COUNTRIES	SPAIN/PORTUGAL	AMERICA
Renaissance Baroque	Renaissance Baroque	Renaissance Plateresque	Early Colonial
Baroque	Baroque	Paleresque Herrara Churriguera	Early Colonial
Baroque 1702-1730 Rococo Neo-Classical	Baroque Rococo	Churrigueresque	William & Mary Queen Anne Georgian American Chippendale Federal
Empire Biedermeier	Empire Neo-Gothic Rococo Revival Historical 'Renaissance'	Fernandino 1814-1833 Isabellino 1833-1870	Empire
Art Nouveau	Art Nouveau		

Introduction

On Collecting Antique Furniture

At some time or another most people own a piece of furniture that is either old or has an appearance that provokes attention beyond its immediate purpose. The piece may have been left to the owner by a relative or friend, they may have picked it up cheaply somewhere on impulse, or they may deliberately have paid a sum of money, more than they would normally pay for a utilitarian piece, simply to have the pleasure and pride of owning something beautiful and unusual.

It is usually just about the time of acquisition, or in contemplation of it, that thoughts occur along the lines of:

What is this piece?
When and where was it made?
Who made it?
Can I obtain similar pieces to keep it company?
Does it matter if it is not in its correct context and setting?

It is for these people, and for those who have not yet even acquired a piece of furniture for the purposes of collecting or for its particular associations that this book is intended. We all use some sort of furniture every day and to justify the idea of collecting pieces of a certain type or style seems unnecessary, but the desire to address the above questions separates the casual acquirer from the true collector. Here, we hope, a start towards most of the answers can be found.

The Scope of this Book

This book is intended as a quick reference work on the furniture of the Western World from the Gothic period of the eleventh century up to the year 1900. It has been designed for both the experienced collector as well as the beginner. We all have to start somewhere and in starting we need to be able to understand the things that interest us not only in the context of history but also in terms of the alternatives and how they came about. We also need to refresh our memory at regular intervals.

For many beginners the styles, the periods and the woods from which furniture has been made seem, initially, confusing. The jargon used – Queen Anne, Louis XVIth, Edwardian Sheraton, Biedermeier, Federal, Empire, Baroque, Gothic – is intimidating. There is, additionally, the question of nationality. Furniture has often travelled far from its origins; at one time it was mostly mobile, hence the Italian word for it: *mobile*. Tastes are very different. From original, roughly-hewn primitives, through the most sophisticated *ébénistes* of the Louis XV/XVI period to the metal and moulded plywood of Charles Eames, there is a long and complex development of design, craftsmanship, style and even political or religious philosophy which ensures that furniture is available to please every sort of collector and every variety of discriminating eye. Keeping track of all these developments is not easy.

This book therefore may seem to have an over-ambitious objective in attempting to cover an enormous subject in its brief pages. This is, however, truly a guide, not an academic study. It concentrates on the facts which we believe to be the most important for any new student of furniture history and which are necessary for any existing collector to use as a reference or refresher to the memory. Where an interest has been roused which needs much deeper satisfaction the reader is advised where to go for more. A comprehensive list of more detailed reference books has been provided in the bibliography.

The illustrations, inevitably, will not be of the exact piece the reader is seeking to identify (unless by extraordinary chance) but they show the source, the period of high fashion, and the factors determining the originality of the piece in enough detail to provide a reasonable understanding of its date and place.

1. What is this piece? In this case it is a very useful Italian walnut and ebonised bureau of c.1750, showing the pretty scrolling of Rococo decoration which emulates the metal mounts of great Louis XV French commodes. The slight shaping to the front and the outset corners are typical of this period.

Where to Start - the Ancient World?

The furniture of the Ancient World is of interest to the archaeologist and scholar but few collectors have the chance of acquiring it. Certain designs and references can be important, however. There are aspects of Ancient Egyptian civilisation, for instance, when many modern cabinetmaking techniques existed, which have been repeated during subsequent periods. Both Greece and Rome owed a great deal to Egyptian creativity. But apart from the thrones of the great, the stools and beds which constituted the major part of the furniture of the ancient world are not significant to us today. The Klismos chair of Greece is the inspiration for the sabre leg chair of the French Empire style, and the Classical Orders of Greece and Rome are vital to the understanding of proportion and the columns and pillars of Classical furniture, but the Renaissance, with its return to Classicism, should provide understanding enough for modern collecting purposes.

2 (Left). What is this piece? Again Italian, but this time from Venice c.1780. Venetian furniture is famous for its painted decoration and this lively chest of drawers is garlanded with floral festoons and an imitation marble top. The straighter line and plain, squarer construction with turned feet emulates the stiffer Louis XVI style which had become fashionable.

3 (Below). A marble headstone of Hegeso showing the Klismos chair of Ancient Greece, with its 'sabre' legs in sweeping curves and the raked back with broad top cross splat for the support of the sitter. This form of chair was inspirational to the French Empire period of c.1800 and its Regency derivative in England.

Why start with Gothic?

For most collectors, the arrival of the Renaissance is seen as being by far an early enough date to consider. But at the Renaissance, which affected Italy most strongly in the beginning, the return of Classicism did not cause the prevailing Gothic style of Northern Europe to evaporate. It lingered for a long time and has returned in some form or another in every period since. The Gothic Period, therefore, is taken as the start point for the modern collector and although dealt with briefly, its significance is quite correctly emphasised.

The Practicalities of Collecting

There are many aspects of the practicalities of collecting antiques – where to buy, how to buy, preservation etc – which might have been dealt with in this book but a multitude of publications already deal in considerable detail with such matters. This Guide is essentially about furniture, its design, its origins and its principal characteristics. The Antique Collectors' Club has always concentrated on explaining pieces which are accessible to the general collector as well as the museum article and the high art available only to the Getty-style collector. This Guide presents a distillation of the most signif-

icant developments in furniture history up to 1900 which are necessary for an understanding of what affected pieces in general use. The styles adopted in vernacular furniture were a direct result of such developments, even though many

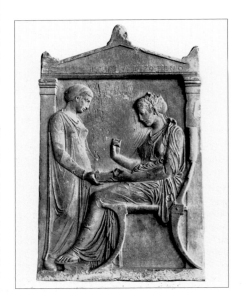

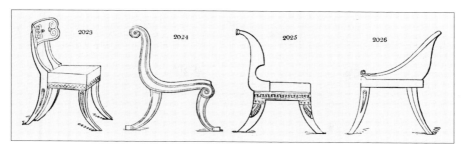

4. Chairs from J.C. Loudon's design book of 1833 showing various 'sabre-leg' chairs of 'Grecian' types described as coming from Thomas Hope's work of 1807. In France such chairs became popular at the start of the Empire period c.1800 and the form was consequently widely adopted across most of Europe.

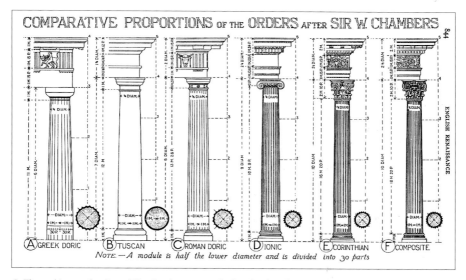

5. The architectural orders of Greek columns were further developed by the Etruscans and the Romans. These orders are of paramount influence and versions of them can be found on much furniture of Classical inspiration.

rural furniture makers were very slow to react. It was in the capital cities and the houses of the rich that new fashions were first displayed; time was to elapse before provincial cabinetmakers and joiners were affected. For this reason only the more significant effects on country and provincial furniture are dealt with here.

We believe the Guide will bring knowledge and enjoyment to everyone who uses it. The reader will be joining a great band of enthusiasts all over the world who are usually only too glad to share their knowledge. More than eighty percent of the members of the Antique Collectors' Club profess themselves to be deeply interested in furniture quite apart from their other interests. Whether or not you enrol in their ranks, we wish you every success with your collection.

1. An oak chest or coffer with Gothic decoration, c.1400. The detail (2) shows how the chest has been embellished with pointed-arch tracery and grotesque animals, both inspired by architectural detail on churches.

2. Detail of oak chest or coffer (1).

CHAPTER 1

The Middle Ages
GOTHIC (1100AD onwards)

The word 'Gothic' was used by the Italian Giorgio Vasari (1511-1574) as a term of reproach for a style which departed from Classical tradition and thus could be compared with those barbarian Goths who had destroyed Rome. It is now used to describe the pointed medieval architecture of the twelfth to the early sixteenth century in Europe, having slowly evolved from the rounded Romanesque.

The style is one of the easiest to distinguish because of the pointed arch, which is said to have originated in the Middle East, possibly Assyria, with Islamic art. The Normans, who conquered England and Jerusalem, also subdued Sicily, where they found the Islamic arch which had been brought there by the Saracens. From the Normans, the thrust of Gothic art in Europe passed to France (see Notre Dame Cathedral, Paris 1163-1235 AD), where it is known as the *Style Ogivale*, and then spread strongly over most of Europe except perhaps Italy, where the Classical influence was never wholly discarded and the Gothic was watered down.

The Gothic has been a perennial style, particularly with religious enthusiasts such as Pugin and the French Troubadour style of the nineteenth century but also with Chippendale in the eighteenth and various English Regency expressions. In Italy it was easily

3. An oak chest of c.1300 with chip-carved roundels of Gothic style taken from church architectural features.

4. An aumbry, or food cupboard/press of c.1500 showing Gothic tracery decoration.

5. A Franco-German oak coffer of the 16th century on which the carved tracery front panels, with their typical ogee arches and rosette enrichments, illustrate many of the principal features of the Gothic style.

6. A Gothic whist-table from Ackermann's Repository of the Arts of 1827, possibly designed by A.W.N. Pugin. Ackermann started publishing illustrations of Gothic furniture in 1810 but the fashion was expensive and this revival of a 15th century version petered out in 1827.

supplanted at the Renaissance (see Chapter 2), but across the rest of Europe into the Middle Ages it was so widely adopted that in Northern Europe it is often difficult to distinguish in which country a medieval piece may have originated. Feudal barons were in a state of semi-continuous warfare so transported much of their furniture from castle to castle, taking chests, beds, chairs and boxes containing clothing, bedding and valuables with them, hence the Italian *mobile* and the French *meuble* to describe furniture. The most important piece of fixed furniture, as in the Ancient World, was the bed.

Furniture decoration, particularly on chests, took the form of carving of the pointed arches and chip-carved roundels similar to the Romanesque. Chairs were also carved in this way – the Coronation Chair at Westminster (thirteenth century) is an example, but Spanish and Portuguese chairs of the thirteenth and fourteenth century show similar decoration. Oak was the principal wood employed in Northern Europe whereas in Southern France, Italy and Spain, walnut, lime, apple, pear, cypress and pine or fir could be used. In Italy the decoration of chests was more frequently painted than carved.

7. A folding X-shaped stool of the 14th century with carved lion decoration. The leather or cloth seat would have been slung between the top rails. Most X stools were much simpler than this.

CHAIRS

The X-shaped chair, stemming from the ancient world, was still in use and was of the folding variety until the fifteenth century and later, when fixed forms of the X-shaped chair with high backs and arms became more common. There were many forms of stools, often with only three legs due to the uneven floors. Sometimes, by continuing the back legs upwards and adding an upper cross piece, the form was developed into what was called a backstool, now indistinguishable from a chair.

CHESTS (TRUNKS)

An early type of chest was made by hollowing out a tree trunk and slicing along the length to make a domed top. From this comes the word trunk for a storage piece. The domed lid ensured that a trunk could only be used for storage and hence it was not as popular as the flat-lidded chest. There was much use of chests or coffers to transport goods; for example, Burgundian chests, or 'Flaunders' chests (Flanders was under Burgundian influence until, c.1500, it became part of Spain's dominions) came into England in large numbers.

LINENFOLD PANELS

The 'linen-fold' carved decoration of panels associated with the style was used from the fifteenth century onwards. Gothic furniture makers at last took a leaf from the stone construction of Gothic churches and used a frame for the main structure instead of solid wood, which enabled thin panels to be used, held in the framework, with carved or painted decoration, the frame forming part of the decorative quality of the piece itself. Grooves, mouldings and panelling were added to by embellishments such as arches, tracery, façades, cusps, trefoil and quatrefoil forms.

The Gothic style had architectural differences in various regions. In Italy it was never strong; in Spain it had Moorish influences such as the horseshoe arch and pierced stone tracery, with much geometrical ornament; in France, where it lasted from 1150 to 1500 AD, it was particularly strong in the Ile de France, or around Paris, spreading out from there. French Gothic cathedrals are short, wide and lofty whereas English ones are long, narrow and low. German Gothic cathedrals follow those of France but in Germany the style took longer to supplant the rounded-arch Romanesque known as Norman in

8. A hutch of the late 16th or early 17th century used for storing corn. The domed top could be lifted off and used as a kneading trough.

9. An English oak chest of c.1540 showing front panels carved with linenfold designs.

10 (Left). A French walnut Gothic revival side cabinet of c.1860-70 again showing the carved tracery decoration true to the Gothic of the 14th-15th century but with some other medieval embellishments of architectural origin.

11 (Opposite). A German walnut Gothic Revival writing cabinet c.1840, with crocketted cornice and doors decorated with carved Gothic tracery of 15th century style.

Britain. In Belgium and Holland a blend of French, German and Spanish influences may be determined owing to the history of the Low Countries, but a remarkable secular development can be established which is in contrast to the religious preponderance elsewhere.

The nineteenth century association of Gothic features with a religious origin has tended to produce a guarded response from collectors. Furniture of a Gothic character, no matter from which period, has inclined towards the preferences of a minority band of collectors who are, none the less, extremely enthusiastic about such pieces.

There was a Gothic revival across Europe most notably around 1830, when much furniture design rather lost its forward impetus and looked backwards, and on through the nineteenth century when a mock-historical taste was catered for in Northern Europe by quite skilled, as well as crass commercial cabinetmakers using mechanical techniques.

CHAPTER 2

The Renaissance (1500-1630AD)
(Classical and Early Baroque styles)

The Renaissance:
literally the rebirth, or revival, in French

The invention of printing spread knowledge and a spirit of enquiry which by the fifteenth century had invigorated intellectual life in Europe. It led to the Reformation in religion and the Renaissance in literature, architecture and the arts. In Italy the Reformation took no hold but there was a revival of ecclesiastical building which caused

The Renaissance used the classical orders in the form of columns and pilasters with mouldings taken from architecture. This is a French 16th century dresser.

a spread of Classic architecture throughout Western Europe in a revolt against medieval – i.e. Gothic – art. The Classic Roman Orders of architecture – Tuscan, Doric, Ionic, Corinthian and Composite – were standardised by architects such as Palladio (hence Palladian and The Palladium) in styles which formed the basis of much modern architecture.

The Renaissance in Italy had its birth in Florence, but Rome and Venice were also important centres. It spread to Spain and France in the sixteenth century and to England over a century or so, where the Gothic slowly yielded, as it did in Germany. By the middle of the seventeenth century fine furniture was Italian Classical in character even though traces of Gothic remained.

The Classical Renaissance
The principal features of the Early Renaissance were:
* a simplicity of outline and detail
* architectural profiles and Classical mouldings
* decorative ornament of acanthus leaf and animal forms
* Roman ornament in the form of columns and pilasters

Because this was initiated in Italy, by the middle of the seventeenth century fine furniture everywhere was based on Italian classic design. However the simplicity soon developed into a richness of ornament and general elaboration which was very quickly adopted in England, France and Flanders, where some Gothic shapes remained, modified by Italian details. It was in the sixteenth and seventeenth century that this exaggeration of ornament led to the Baroque.

Baroque
(see also Chapter 3 – The 17th Century)
In contrast to the rather still and severe classic ideal, Baroque art is curved, fantastic and irregular. Twisted columns, broken pediments, outsized mouldings and other excesses take the eye away from structure and on to a more theatrical appearance. In furniture there was a tendency to overload the base and upper parts with carving or pediments. Scrolling and carving gave a sculptural effect to many pieces. Surface treatment was elaborate too, with inlays, painting, gilding and marquetry. Marble and imitation stonework, colourful textiles, metal, tortoiseshell and caning all added more complex visual treatment. It was an art form which endured for almost two centuries across Europe.

1. A walnut Italian Savonarola-type armchair of a kind made in Italy from the Renaissance onwards, featuring the X-shape below hooped arm supports and back which is the hallmark of this and the 'Dante' chair. Also known as a 'curule' shape. Fitted, in this case, with iron hoops for carrying bars. (This is a 16th/17th century example).

ITALY
---

1. Early Renaissance – Quattrocento (1400-1500)
In the early part of the Renaissance in Italy there was a renewed interest in Classical forms. Large pieces like chests and cupboards had architectural bases, pillars and cornices. The bases were solid to the floor, without feet. Forms of chest, especially the *cassone*, which dated from the pre-Renaissance period, were still made from the solid, well after France had developed on to framed-panel construction.

The *cassapanca* was a *cassone* with added back and sides to form a settee. The *credenza* – an Italian credence table or cabinet – was of religious origin (from *credere*, to believe) and was at first a side table of Gothic style, but developed into a low sideboard with doors and drawers.

Chairs tended to be straight and rectangular, but the X-shape of the Savonarola and the Dante chairs was also used, derived from Moorish and, even further back, Egyptian origins.

Tables were trestle type derivations with turned baluster legs or shaped end slabs, but there were four-legged types with box stretchers. As in all periods, beds were considered important items but the climate was not suitable for the Northern enclosed bed so a lighter four-post type with Oriental fabrics would be used.

Throughout the fifteenth and sixteenth centuries it can be said that Italian furniture was usually made of walnut, oiled or waxed to a deep colour fairly simply ornamented to start with but increasingly more sophisticated towards the end of the period, with paint and inlay giving way to carving architectural in proportion, designed for large rooms, even quite cumbersome

There were distinct regional types in Italy:

2. A cassone *of carved walnut with gilt painting of c.1600. The domed top has fluted mouldings and the lower part has a cartouche in the centre. The paw feet are original. The bun feet below them are later.*

3. A Florentine cassone *of walnut with parquetry inlay, late 15th century. A sophisticated piece with an intarsia pictorial panel of the Piazza Santa Croce and carved scrolls, wings and flowerheads, raised on hoof feet.*

4. A cassapanca – *a* cassone *with back and sides added to make a settee – of 16th century date, with carved lozenge shape, on a gadrooned base.*

5. A cassone *with* certosina *inlays, 16th century, either from Lombardy or Venice. This bone inlay on a dark background is of Islamic origin and appears in Spain and elsewhere.*

6. *A Renaissance walnut and marquetry table from Tuscany, c.1580, with carved scrolls, reeded columns, masks, grotesque birds and seated lion feet. Tables of this type, with arcaded pillars running lengthwise below the top, were reproduced as 'Renaissance' tables in the 19th century.*

Tuscany, centred on Florence, was a leading
    producer of refined and restrained pieces
Rome, particularly after 1500, developed richly
    carved furniture
Genoa and Liguria were known for four-door
    cupboards
Siena was noted for painted and gilded
    decoration
Lombardy was associated with *certosina* inlays
    – these are of ivory or bone on a dark wood

or ebonised background, of possibly Islamic
origin, and are found in Spain (sometimes
called Moorish from their Arabic origin) and
Venice as well. Even in the nineteenth
century, Milan and Lombardy produced big
cabinets with this decoration
Venice, at the start of the period, was producing
inlaid furniture but later took to making the
highly decorative painted pieces now
usually celebrated as Venetian.

7. A Bolognese walnut table/cupboard of c.1580 showing simple lozenge mouldings on the two lower doors and the end shaping found in Southern Europe at the time.

8. A Tuscan walnut credenza, *late 16th century, with two doors below a frieze containing two drawers, the frieze guilloche carved and the cupboard doors flanked by fluted pilasters. The lower apron is also fluted.*

2. Later Renaissance – Cinquecento (High Renaissance) 1500-1600

During the Later Renaissance the rooms became smaller, cushions were used to alleviate the rather severe nature of the seating, a wider variety of tables was constructed, animal feet were put on chests and sideboards made their appearance.

During this period the carved decoration was developed which used nearly all the forms which are now part of the furniture expert's vocabulary, especially where floral and Classical decoration are concerned. These are detailed opposite.

VOCABULARY OF
RENAISSANCE FEATURES

Over and again, in books and particularly in auctioneers' descriptions, words are used to describe design features which occur repeatedly on furniture, mainly of Classical inspiration. These can be mystifying to the new collector and some of the principal ones illustrated in the pages which follow are listed for clarification as follows:

acanthus leaf – the acanthus is a prickly-leaved plant and the leaf was used in Greek architectural decoration. It is one of the most heavily-used motifs, right on into the nineteenth century

animal forms – birds, lion masks, hoof feet, etc. These have been popular as decoration ever since the Renaissance

broken pediment – this is a straight or swan-neck pediment (the triangular top over a cabinet etc) which is broken – i.e. does not meet – at the centre or apex

cartouche – an unrolled scroll or oval tablet with edges rolled over

caryatid – a female figure used as a support instead of a column

fluting – hollows or channels cut in columns

gadrooning – carved edge ornament in short convex flutes or ruffles

gargoyles – grotesque figures

guilloche – a continuous running or band ornament of interlacing circles

intarsia – inlaid decoration of a pictorial type

paterae – small round or oval carved ornaments

pilasters – rectangular or half-round pillars

reeding – inverted fluting i.e. adding long parallel raised mouldings like reeds to columns and elsewhere, giving a parallel-ridged effect

rinceaux – continuous ornament of scroll, spiral or wavy form

1. A French Renaissance oak cupboard of the 16th century, showing carved decoration in which there is a good deal of Gothic embellishment in the linenfold, roundel and floral motifs.

rosettes – rose shaped paterae or discs

strapwork – carved surface bands or panels with interlacing effects

term figure – a column, plinth or pillar with the top carved as a human head or pagan god, the lower trunk diminishing into a kind of sheath

There were many other devices, but the above are those which occur most frequently.

FRANCE

---

1. The Early Renaissance – François 1 (1515-1547)

In Renaissance France there was an immediate impact on furniture from developments in Italy but this was assimilated into a domestic style, with influences from Spanish-Islamic work and German and Flemish detailing. As in Italy,

2 (Left). A Renaissance oak coffer c.1570 with carved allegorical panel flanked by figures to the front and corners. The ends are decorated with strapwork.

3 (Above). A Henri II walnut cupboard of c.1550 in which the architectural Classicism of the pillar or column supports acts as a façade to a cupboard above a drawer, carved with a figure of Venus Marina and exotic beasts.

4. A French Renaissance walnut cabinet, c.1580, with doors above and below, elaborately carved with masks, foliage, scroll-work, birds and term figures.

walnut, waxed to a deep colour, predominated. There was much surface carving and the use of ebony was so valued that it was from this period and ever since that a fine cabinetmaker was referred to as an *ébéniste*.

At first French Renaissance furniture is Gothic, with carved Classical details such as Romayne panels (or carved portrait medallions)

5. A walnut French court cupboard of c.1580 showing strongly-reeded columns, gadrooning and, on the back panels, strapwork and oval paterae.

imposed on it. Dressoirs and credence cabinets show such decoration, gradually assimilating Classical columns and similar Italian features.

The table received much more attention, changing from a utilitarian piece into a more ornamental structure. Beds received more carved decoration. Chairs of smaller size were developed, some with straw seats, and the dress of women suggested armless chairs to cope with the current fashions or chairs like the *caquetoire* (a gossip's chair), which had shorter arms to provide more space for the materials enveloping the sitter.

2. The High Renaissance – Henri II, Catherine of Medici, François II, Henri III and IV (1550-1610)

The style of François I gradually developed into

more Classical features but in the country and provinces Gothic still persisted. It was a violent period of religious upheaval and changes were rapid. In the provinces a richer middle class emerged, giving rise to locally-made furniture imitating town examples in local woods, hence the French Provincial furniture (or *Mobilier Rustique*) of great charm which has its devoted collectors.

The *armoire à deux corps*, or double-bodied cupboard, had an upper section of less width than the lower and was often decorated with Classical pillars as well as flat carving. Broken pediments were used as well as cartouches and flat strapwork. Table bases also used columns, balusters, caryatids and scrollwork. One of the most famous 'huchiers' was Hugues Sambrin of Dijon, the

6. A French oak dressoir of the late 16th century showing Renaissance features in the mask-carved frieze, the panelled doors carved with figures of saints – the central one below an eagle – and arcaded fluted column supports. The drawers below the cupboard doors are also carved with lion mask handles.

capital of Burgundy, who published plates on the use of the architectural orders on furniture in 1572.

Chairs were rather stiff, straight and rectangular, as in Italy, with architectural columns also being used on important seating.

SPAIN

1. Mudejar (1250-1500)

In the sixteenth century Spain was in a position of world dominance but its furniture, as in most periods, reflected strong foreign influences. Until 1500 Spain was known for *Mudejar* furniture, which was of Moorish inspiration. The Moors did not produce furniture of Western type, using cushions for seating and low platforms for tables. When they were expelled in 1492 more European influences prevailed and Gothic architecture, with Moorish decoration, appeared. In furniture, walnut, pine, cedar and olive were used with inlaying of mother-of-pearl, metals, and other woods. Star patterns and intricate geometric designs of Islamic type – literally arabesques – provided distinctive ornamentation. Leather was used on seats in stamped, tooled, embossed, gilded and painted finishes.

1. A papeleira *– a* vargueño *without the fall front – of mudejar style with Moorish inlays, raised on an arcaded somewhat Romanesque stand with turned columns and flat end frame plinths. A traditional piece but actually a modern reproduction.*

2. A painted and parcel gilt walnut vargueño *on chest, shown open to reveal the numerous drawers inside, gilded and painted with flowers. The chest is possibly of later date; many* vargueños *have lost their original column-legged understructures due to the ravages of time.*

2. Plateresque (1500-1556)

At the time of the Early Renaissance, *Mudejar* gave way to the Italian influences brought about by the close ties between the two countries through the Pope. Plateresque comes from the word *platero* – a silversmith – since this metal was pre-eminent during Spain's domination of the Netherlands, Austria and Germany at the time of Carlos V. There was some interchange with Flemish styles because of this.

Spanish furniture was heavy and crudely made, sometimes with obvious nailed construction. Polychrome painting covered many blemishes and turning was repetitive. Walnut, pine, oak, chestnut, cedar and pear were used with metal ornament, inlays, chip gouging and similarly crude forms of carving.

Metal supports were used on the underside of the well-known Spanish table, usually a splayed trestle form, the wrought iron stretchers having decorative twists or scrolls. The trestle ends could be square, turned or pierced and the thick tops are usually square cut.

On square Spanish chairs of the period the upholstery is often simple stretched leather secured by prominent nails. The X-chair was common as was the ladderback.

The important Spanish cabinet was the *vargueño* (said to come from Vargas), a desk box with a fall front, mounted on a support composed of pillars, double or triple, with an arched colonnade between. Inside the desk box there were many small drawers, which could be decorated with paint or inlays. The drop flap had pierced iron mounts and hinges and hasp were decorative metalwork as well.

3. Herrera (1556-1600)

Philip II succeeded Carlos V in 1556 and his architect, Herrera, gave his name to a more severe style which came about as a reaction to the richness of the High Renaissance. Herrera is an austere style also known as *desornamentado* – literally unornamented – which was eventually superseded by the counter-reaction of Churriguera in the Baroque period.

1. A Flemish oak press of c.1540 in which the decoration takes the form of Romayne panels of portrait medallions which were a feature of the Renaissance. Similar decoration is to be found all over Europe.

THE LOW COUNTRIES

The Gothic style prevailed until, in the sixteenth century, having been under Burgundian influence, Flanders came under Spanish rule and was therefore exposed to Mediterranean Renaissance influences somewhat before other Northern European countries. There was also an Italian influence emanating from France and Southern Germany, so that the Gothic in due course became modified by Classical decoration.

Antwerp, Brussels and Liège were important furniture centres, Antwerp eventually becoming noted for fine veneered, tortoiseshell and painted cabinets (see seventeenth century). In the early Renaissance distinctive cupboards came from Flanders, with panels carved in low relief with an X-form. By the middle of the sixteenth century the Classical orders were in use and Renaissance decoration appeared, particularly in the northern Dutch Republic, which had split off

2. A Flemish oak cupboard of the early 17th century which by contrast shows how the Classical orders of the Renaissance had now spread to include fluted Ionic columns, scrolling foliage, birds and lion masks.

from the Catholic South after bitter religious wars. In Holland a cabinet called a *beeldenkast* was made, decorated with carved scenes and figures, but this was for rich clients, and the work was divided between cabinetmaker, who constructed the piece, and carver, who produced the elaborate figures.

Although not as splendid as Italy or France, houses in the Low Countries did contain furniture of substantial and well-made characteristics.

GERMANY

There is a distinct line of demarcation between Northern and Southern Germany in furniture terms, due to both the influences of outside styles and the woods available.

Before the Renaissance, in the North oak was used and styles followed Scandinavian influences in Gothic, Romanesque, Celtic and Byzantine designs. In the South fir and pine were

1. A four-poster bed of c.1580 from the Schloss Amberg, Souther Germany, made of purplewood inlaid with ebony and ivory.

2. A Nuremberg cupboard made of oak and ash, dated 1541, showing Renaissance decoration and architectural formality.

used and the influence was Italian, with Gothic carved ornament and green and red paint.

The cities of Southern Germany traded freely with Northern Italy and the Renaissance made its first appearance in the South, where cupboards of Lombardy type, with Classical ornament, soon appeared. Veneered panels of walnut enriched the pine and fir surfaces and more elaborate joinery, with mitring, broken corners and serpentine mouldings was used instead of carving.

The North moved much more slowly away from the Gothic, and oak furniture continued to be made well into the sixteenth century, when Cologne and Munster, important centres of Northern cabinetmaking, started to use Classical forms. German beds and cabinets of the sixteenth century show the use of architectural features and intarsia panels of Renaissance inspiration, which remained popular on into the eighteenth century.

3. A German walnut chest dated 1551 in Italian Renaissance style with inlaid architectural decorative views.

1. A walnut caquetoire *(gossip's) chair of English make, taken from a French form, c.1622. The back bears the arms of the city of New Sarum – Salisbury. The turned column supports are fluted.*

2. An oak English chest of c.1540 with linenfold panels forming the decoration. The main frame would be of joined construction, allowing lighter panels to be inserted.

3. An oak and walnut English joined centre table with folding top c.1580. Note the more sophisticated legs, with fluting and gadrooning.

ENGLAND

Tudor (1485-1603)

The Gothic style, with linenfold panelling and other distinctive characteristics, had become well entrenched in England and oak was used extensively as the wood for this furniture. The Oak Period is a term used for furniture up to 1660

and Gothic was its main source, although Italian influences began to be felt, firstly in architecture. As with other countries, the Classical detailing came before any major change, for instance with Romayne panels (portrait carvings) being imposed on existing pieces.

Tudor roses, dolphins, scrolls and similar Renaissance decoration appeared on Gothic

5. A late Elizabethan oak court cupboard of c.1600 with floral inlay and perspective architectural panel, using holly or box for the light colours. The carved decoration includes masks, arched panels, strapwork and a dentil moulding in the frieze under the top. Clustered columns replace the bulbous turning of the normal Elizabethan pillars – the Renaissance influence is evident.

pieces, producing a particular Elizabethan style, which also had bulbous turned uprights and square, low stretchers between members. Inlays of ebony, holly, box and sycamore were used. The furniture included panelled chairs, draw tables, court cupboards (named from the French *court*, or short, since it was a low cupboard), large beds with heavy wooden canopies, many chests and coffers with carved decoration. After 1500 panelled construction superseded the boarded type.

An alternative to the heavy, panelled 'wainscot' chair was a *caquetoire* or *caqueteuse* chair based on the French (q.v.) model, and the X-chair and a turned or 'thrown' chair, with its triangular seat.

The more tolerant ambience of England brought over many Continental workers and

some of their styles were absorbed. Woods such as walnut, chestnut, beech and fir became alternatives to oak and painted surfaces gave way to waxed finishes.

4. A joined oak court cupboard (court from the French word for low) or buffet of c.1600 with elaborately carved figure and animal supports.

CHAPTER 3

The 17th Century

The seventeenth century saw the Baroque style come into fashion, initially as a grandiloquent expression of the importance of Italian city states, which were gradually overtaken by a unified France. The pompous and impressive nature of the Baroque ensured that it was soon taken up by any powerful or rich person wishing to emphasise a position, but its ornamental features were used on more modest pieces as a reflection of high fashion.

1. The height of the Baroque – a late 17th century Neapolitan ebony and tortoiseshell cabinet on stand, mounted with plated panels under glass. The cabinet is of breakfront architectural form and has cupboards and drawers painted with mythological and allegorical scenes. The stand illustrates some of the most extravagant fancies of the Baroque – supporting blackamoors wearing feathered tunics, a central waisted cartouche, scrolled acanthus leaves and lions.

2. Another example of the 17th century Italian Baroque – a Genoese cabinet on a stand, this time supported on caryatid blackamoors and paw feet. The cabinet is painted and embellished with parcel-gilt (meaning partly-gilded) and has doors and drawers faced by figures and busts. The scrolled cresting to the top has a pair of cherubs at the centre.

ITALY

Baroque 1560-1700

Italian Baroque is possibly the most exaggerated style of all. Its exuberant decoration is the logical outcome of High Renaissance development taken to excess. The Renaissance features are over-emphasised in the form of ornate broken pediments, twirled scrolls, twisted turnings and lavish carving in what seems like a frantic desire to impress regardless of form. (The period 1560 to 1800 is sometimes referred to as 'Decadenza' in Italy.)

The restrained outlines of classical architecture are smothered by ornamentation, inlays and theatrical effects, sometimes said to be effected in an attempt to show the power and wealth of the Catholic Church to impress waverers towards Protestantism. On the other hand, there were some immensely wealthy families in Italy at this period and the style undoubtedly suited those wishing to astonish with their opulence.

Baroque furniture was used not only in Italy but in other European countries for state apartments and grand houses or salons. Usually this furniture formed part of a lavish

3. A slightly later walnut credenza than the previous example in Chapter 2 in which the side columns are turned and there are cartouches and gadrooned decoration c.1600.

4. Not all Italian furniture of the 17th century was so elaborate. This walnut writing table of c.1660 shows supports which have been influenced by Renaissance-Baroque scrolling but retains a simple basic form. It is allied to another Mediterranean form – the Spanish table in which the curved central stretcher-supports are made of wrought iron.

overall design including walls, ceilings, mirrors, candelabra and so on, making individual pieces difficult to cope with out of context. Gradually the Italian Baroque accepted elements from other countries and the big cabinets, console tables and wall benches it generated, with their supporting and pendent cherubs, mermaids, lions, eagles and blackamoors, surrounded by scrolls shells and leaves, could be gilded or painted to strike the eye as forcefully as possible. Multicoloured marble, scagliola and pietra dura were all used for the tops of tables and chests. It was a profuse and extravagant style which has since been much revived and adapted.

Architecture and sculpture were highly influential on furniture design, especially in the larger pieces. The cassone was gradually superseded by the wardrobe and the chest of drawers. The ornamental side table, known as a console table, came into great popularity and was made in lavish manner, with marble tops on increasingly sumptuous bases in which sculpture appears to have been more important than structure. The same applied to ornamental chairs and thrones made more for show than use

5. A marble-topped Roman giltwood side table of bold Baroque-Rococo extravagance c.1700, the cabriole legs joined by an arched stretcher of pierced, ornate design. This popular exuberance has been much copied since.

6. Late 17th century Italian walnut armchair with scrolled arms, front legs and stretchers with central finial which give more than a hint of the scrolled decoration of the Rococo which followed the Baroque style. The velvet coverings are replacements.

or comfort, but these were not typical of seating furniture, which was increasingly of a more upholstered and comfortable character.

Lacquer was used as a surface finish for smaller pieces of furniture, particularly in Venice, where chinoiserie decorated with gilt was used, although not much has survived.

Pietra dura – literally hard stone – involving a pattern of semi-precious stones such as agate, lapis lazuli, porphyry and marbles was employed as a decoration on cabinets and other pieces rather like mosaic. Visiting foreigners were much impressed with this pietra dura work and bought many pieces to be shipped back to their own countries. The demand continued and it has been used as decoration on into the nineteenth century.

The Baroque style, which essentially came from Italy, was soon to be adopted in France, especially in the later part of the seventeenth century when Louis XIV's glittering court was at the full height of its magnificence.

FRANCE

1. Louis XIII 1610-1643 (High or Late Renaissance)

The reign of Louis XIII began with him as a minor and Marie de Medici effectively in power. Due to the wars, foreign influences were strong, especially Flemish ones, perhaps due to de Medici's taste for Flemish art. Large numbers of Flemish immigrants came into Paris and the provinces as a result.

The High Renaissance came to its climax during this period and decoration became profuse. Although walnut and ebony were the principal woods used, the surfaces and structures incorporated panels, columns and marquetry, which had come from the Low

1. Not all Louis XIV furniture was grandiloquent. These charming walnut guéridons – a guéridon is technically a small table, but these were probably used as candlestick stands – with hexagonal tops and bases with ebonised circles show the delightful twist and baluster turning which was a feature of later Baroque furniture. Similar small tables were produced in other countries during the same period.

2. A simple walnut table of Louis XIII period c.1640 which has much in common with Anglo-Dutch/Flemish designs of later in the century. The tray top with drawer below is supported on octagonal tapering legs which are joined by a curved and finialled 'X' stretcher. The bun feet are later replacements but are correct in design.

43

3. The work of André-Charles Boulle (1642-1732) has been celebrated since his creation of this form of decorative inlay using metals such as silver and brass together with tortoiseshell. This is a commode, a word used by Bérain to describe a form of chest of drawers in 1708, of a more lavish Boulle type c.1700 in which the top is inlaid with with figures of musicians and a scene from a masque. The hoof feet are decorated with leaf forms as well.

Countries. Tortoiseshell and gilt bronze surfaces on some pieces contrasted with rich Flemish style carving and many applied turnings with complex profiles on others. Geometric panelling with deep mouldings, again probably of Flemish influence, is also very characteristic.

Louis XIII's queen was Anne of Austria, who in turn was influenced by Cardinal Mazarin, a patron of the arts. Mazarin inclined towards Italian work and the taste for foreign luxuries enabled many Italian and German pieces to be imported into the grand houses.

2. Louis XIV 1643-1715 (Baroque)

The reign of Louis XIV saw the rise of France to great power. The style of Louis XIV is distinctively Baroque, a style which emanated from Italy and which is described above. Carving and decoration in the form of animals, natural foliage and beasts of mythology were used. Woods were richer than the oak, walnut and ebony of the previous period; there was much marquetry and other inlays. It was the period of the great André-Charles Boulle, the producer of inlaid marquetry of tortoiseshell, brass, horn, pewter, tin, ivory, bone and mother-

4. This form of desk is called a Bureau Mazarin *after the influential Cardinal of that name. This example, c.1690, is a floral and strapwork marquetry version (they were often Boulle) on eight parcel-gilt typical square tapering legs joined by 'X' stretchers. There are seven bow-fronted drawers and a bow-fronted cupboard under the central drawer.*

5. This is a Louis XIV commode, showing how the later form of Louis XV and XVI developed. It has a marble top, is bow-fronted and the front feet are created by extending the canted and fluted corners down to the ground, then embellishing them with metal mounts. The surfaces are of kingwood parquetry in straightforward quarterings surrounding by cross-banding.

of-pearl in intricate detail which has borne that name ever since and has been much reproduced.

The Chinese taste (see Chapter 6) was indulged in, starting with porcelain and then lacquering of surfaces to a high varnish known as *Vernis-Martin*, after Martin's process.

The ornate console table from Italy became popular and, by developing the table with drawers or the coffer on legs fitted with drawers, *commodes* – chests of drawers of curved or straight fronts – made their appearance, to be much developed later. Boulle is also credited

6. Regional furniture forms an important part of the range of French production. This is an armoire from Alsace c.1700 which has elements in common with German cabinets of the same period, particularly in the arched panelled niches in the doors and the bobbin-turned columns. There is geometrical parquetry, scroll-cresting topped by masks and a panelled frieze. The base has a drawer in it.

with the invention of this piece which gradually superseded the cabinet towards the end of the century. A writing table of pedestal type supported on eight legs, now known as a Bureau Mazarin after the great Cardinal, often decorated with Boulle inlays, made its appearance and could also be used as a dressing table.

The comfort offered by chairs increased, with seats becoming lower and backs higher. Some had curved arm rests with a pad and the X-stretcher between the scrolled or turned legs was of curved form. The wood could be gilded or painted and towards the end of the century wing armchairs made their appearance.

SPAIN

At the start of the seventeenth century Italian Baroque came to Spain and was treated with local variations. An architect called Churriguera gave his name to the *Churrigueresque* style, which was of Baroque extravagance, suiting the pomp and ceremony of a great power with even greater global ambitions. There were three reigns during the century, Philip III, Philip IV and Carlos II, but crisis dogged the country and the Thirty Years War and conflict with the growing might of France ended the century badly.

The influence of Italy and France on Spanish Baroque produced highly ornamented pieces and the *vargueño* of the rich home in the previous century now became much more

1 . A walnut 17th century Spanish vargueño *with an elaborately carved front enclosing an ivory-inlaid interior, on an oak stand of typical arcaded pillaring.*

2. A Spanish oak refectory table in which the elements of scrolled Baroque influence are evident. It has four drawers under the top and the carved decoration includes bird-heads, masks and angels. The six scrolled legs are united by pierced carved stretchers with a central cherub (or putto) mask flanked by leaf-scrolls. The scrolled feet are also typical – such folded feet or scrolled feet are often referred to as Spanish feet.

3. A simpler Spanish walnut table with scrolled end supports and typical curved iron stretchers below. Late 17th century but made from then ever onwards.

widespread, but the supports changed from arcaded columns to the turned and twisted legs of the Baroque. Ivory inlays and gilding were used as well as tortoiseshell. Another type of cabinet known as a *papeleira*, without the fall front of the *vargueño*, but with similar decoration, also became popular.

The simple chest remained in lesser households but was discarded by the well-to-do in favour of a trunk with a domed top covered in leather or velvet and having pierced metal mounts.

The trestle table was still in use, with Baroque variations to the leg designs and ornamental

4. A Spanish chair of 17th century type with a rectangular back and square legs. The arms end in scrolls but otherwise it is a very simple chair. Such chairs, covered in various textiles or in leather were made for many years and still are.

5. A Spanish mother-of-pearl and tortoiseshell inlaid cabinet on stand of the later 17th century, showing traditional decorative Moorish influences but using flowers and foliage rather than the formal patterns of Islam. The spirally-turned legs show Baroque influences.

wrought-iron stretchers. A table with drawers under the frieze, on turned legs, with flared mouldings between drawers, is also typical.

Chairs with twist-turned legs and stretchers, with seats and backs of stretched leather, took the place of the simple, earlier form in which

6. A later 17th century vargueño in which the later stand is of simple column supports strengthened by scrolled iron stretchers. The geometrical drawers and doors are carved and parcel-gilded.

uprights and stretchers were of square section. Versions of scroll-legged Louis XIII chairs were also made, properly upholstered and covered in fabric or leather. Caning, introduced from Portugal, was used for some high-backed chairs of the period.

7. Not all Spanish furniture was elaborate as a vargueño. This walnut chest of drawers of c.1700 with carrying handles is decorated with incised carving and mouldings in geometric panels of a kind seen in other parts of Europe.

PORTUGAL

Portugal became independent of Spain in 1640 but a period of austerity was required and so foreign influences were not as strong as those in Spain. A more local, self-contained development began to take place. For instance, at the start of the century chairs were of Spanish Renaissance type, but in the second half Portugal produced its own chair, which subsequently was copied in Spain. This was a chair having a high, arched back, turned legs and side stretchers, but with an elaborately carved front stretcher, usually pierced and scrolled. In Portugal this chair was on turned feet but a version with scrolled feet was known as *pie de pincel* in Spain where, as in Portugal, embossed leather coverings were also used, fastened by large brass nails. The wood was initially walnut or oak, later becoming jacaranda or pausanto from Brazil, which was recaptured from the Dutch in 1654. Dutch chairs of embossed leather in this period are the result of Portuguese influence.

The cabinet called a *contador* was developed around mid-century. This was yet again an open cabinet with many drawers like a Spanish *papeleira* but it sometimes had ripple or wave mouldings of Dutch inspiration, known as *tremidos,* and stood on elaborately turned legs. Although the chest had been superseded by the trunk in the sophisticated parts of Spain it was used in Portugal for much longer.

Lacquer furniture of Oriental style, resulting from Portugal's long association with the East, was also prevalent, usually cupboards or cabinets coloured in red, black or green with gold highlights.

Northern Portuguese furniture of carved and rustic style, with leaf decoration and heraldic crests, similar to that of Northern

1. A Portuguese chair which was influential in Spain. This walnut version, c.1680, shows the turned legs and stretchers, and the particular high, arched back and the carved front stretcher between the front legs, scrolled and sometimes pierced, that was of Portuguese origin. This chair is covered in tooled and embossed leather nailed to the frame by brass nails, which is also found in the Spanish copies.

Spain and frequently using chestnut, was made from this period over the next 100 years.

1. This 17th century Flemish oak armoire shows the strong Renaissance features which spread from Flanders to other countries, i.e. fluted Ionic columns, masks, scroll and floral work and elaborate arched panels. It does not, however, divert a great deal from late 16th century designs and gives little hint of the glorious Antwerp cabinets which soon eclipsed this work in fame.

THE LOW COUNTRIES

This was a period of great influence for the Low Countries, in particular the new Dutch Republic which became a great maritime power. Craftsmen from both Northern and Southern Netherlands travelled widely across Europe and were employed by the great courts, so that, for example, Flemish influence was particularly strong in France and the Mortlake tapestry factory in England depended on Flemish weavers.

The cabinetmakers of the Low Countries were highly skilled at veneering and the Dutch involvement in the Far East (see Chapter 4) added exotic woods, materials and designs to their repertoire. Lacquering, painting, marquetry, tortoiseshell, mother-of-pearl and other decorative finishes were used to the great admiration of the French, English, German and other wealthy clients much further afield.

The Baroque style spread via Flanders, especially to cabinet pieces of architectural character such as four-door cupboards of oak panelled with ebony, the cornices being adorned with cartouches and foliage. Antwerp cabinets on stands veneered with ebony or tortoiseshell or ivory were sometimes supported by caryatids and were of large scale at the start of the period

2. Still very much in an oak country tradition. This Dutch or Flemish table, with its hugely bulbous leg embellishments, is of a type typical of the Low Countries in the 17th century. Some of them were 'draw' tables, i.e. the top could be extended by pulling out two lower panels.

3. Dutch ebony and rosewood cupboard of c.1660 with the elaborately-moulded panelling associated with Holland and Ionic pillars to the corners. The frieze and the drawer below are carved with leaf scrolls.

but became much more simplified by the end of the seventeenth century.

The side table supported on scrolled supports of carved decoration appeared and spread rapidly from Flanders to other regions. Floral marquetry, following the work of Golle, the Dutch *ébéniste* to Louis XIV, who made a cabinet for Mazarin (q.v.), became a Dutch speciality. It tended to be more florid than the work of Boulle (q.v.) and imposes itself on the furniture to the extent of detracting from the structural lines. Deep mouldings are very

4. An Antwerp cabinet on stand of c.1685 showing the remarkable sophistication of such pieces – this is by no means as Baroque as some versions, which could have caryatid or animal supports of Neapolitan extravagance. In this case the cabinet is ebonised but with tortoiseshell and gilt metal decoration and incorporates floral scrolls, a cabochon, musical putti, ivory balusters, caryatids, pilasters etc etc. It is suggested that the gilded stand with its octagonal tapering legs is a later restoration.

5. The name of Daniel Marot is used to describe walnut dining chairs of this Flemish type of c.1690 since the pierced leaf and scroll cresting above a pierced curved and carved splat, plus the velvet seats and the scroll-carved cabriole legs ending in hoof feet, let alone the leaf-carved scrolled cross stretchers are work for which the Frenchman, who worked under Boulle before emigrating to Holland to escape religious persecution, was celebrated.

6. By the end of the 17th century Holland was becoming celebrated for marquetry work of the floral type seen on this centre table raised on ebonised, spirally-turned legs joined by a flat X-stretcher.

characteristic and twist turning, oval bulb legs and bun feet were equally popular.

Daniel Marot, who was related to Golle, worked in Holland where he produced beds, tables and a chair with a high back which tends to bear his name (5). The Dutch Baroque cabinet appeared, with chamfered sides, drawers below of straight or bombé form and a glazed upper section in which Chinese or Delft porcelain and pottery could be displayed under the typical Dutch-gabled pediment above. This piece, either plain, walnut-veneered or decorated with marquetry, became irrevocably a symbol of Dutch furniture and was much produced in the subsequent century. It has been reproduced ever since.

7. This form of caned Flemish carved walnut armchair with scrollwork, spiral turning and pierced scrollwork front stretcher is of a type which was popular and spread to England with the return of Charles II at the Restoration.

1. This German parquetry cupboard of c.1660 may be compared with the Alsace armoire in the French section (page 46). Its arched panel doors and the bobbin turned or ribbed columns have common features with the Alsace version although there are some differences of detail; this piece lacks the scroll-cresting topped by masks.

2. A South German marquetry inlaid side cabinet of the early 17th century with arched panelled doors inlaid with figures of warriors wearing feathered helmets and flowing robes. Under the top there are two drawers inlaid with foliate strapwork.

GERMANY

In this Baroque period the Italian and later the French influence was strong throughout Germany, where the differentiation between North and South was still noticeable. In the North, the Hanseatic ports such as Hamburg and Bremen traded with Scandinavia, where Sweden had been ruled by German princes but was subject to Dutch influences in design. Denmark was also under German princely influence and similarly felt the strong influences from the Low Countries.

Frankfurt was an important centre for the production of cabinets and cup-

3. More warriors in arched panels – a South German marquetry cabinet of c.1610, this time with an upper section with term figure supports and cupboards inlaid with scenes from the story of Judith and Holofernes. The shape of the piece will be familiar to collectors of Northern European oak cupboards and presses of later date.

boards following earlier Dutch Baroque lines but eventually more enriched and luxurious in both outline and style. Both Frankfurt and Hamburg were centres which towards the end of the century produced walnut cupboards of architectural form with heavy cornices and

57

4. A marquetry cabinet from Augsburg or Ulm of c.1610 with doors inlaid with architectural fantasy towers. Inside, there are drawers and small cupboards. The stand with spirally-turned legs and X-stretcher is not original but is of a type conforming to the top.

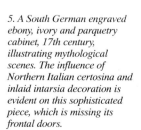

5. A South German engraved ebony, ivory and parquetry cabinet, 17th century, illustrating mythological scenes. The influence of Northern Italian certosina and inlaid intarsia decoration is evident on this sophisticated piece, which is missing its frontal doors.

6. A late 17th century German marquetry centre table of a type influenced by Low Countries and French Louis XIV work, with perhaps rather cumbersome ring-turned tapering fluted legs with gadrooned collars. These legs, joined by an X-stretcher, are of period type but may be replacements.

much carved ornament of masks, naturalistic and scroll motifs. North German cupboards became increasingly simplified towards the end of the century.

In the South, Munich and Augsburg reacted to Italian influences together with Nuremberg, producing pieces of Baroque splendour. The veneer work of South German examples is excellent and is allied to the best intarsia panels of Italy.

59

1. A later, more restrained form of Early Jacobean English court cupboard c.1620 in which the pillars are less bulbous than Elizabethan examples and the carving is all fairly low relief. The panels still use the lozenge or diamond shape and arching.

ENGLAND

Early Jacobean 1603-1649
Cromwellian or Commonwealth 1649-1660
Restoration Stuart
(or Carolean after Charles II) 1660-1685
Late Jacobean 1685-1688
William and Mary 1688-1702

At the start of the seventeenth century the Renaissance in England was still modified by the underlying Gothic (Elizabethan) style which had prevailed in the sixteenth century. Under James I and Charles I the furniture started to become lighter, less bulbous and Renaissance-classical motifs such as Ionic columns, acanthus leaves, guilloches and so on were used in ornament. Gateleg tables came into use and more upholstery was used on chairs, which varied from Renaissance types to those with turned members. The X-chair of Italian type was also prevalent.

The Civil War had the effect of bringing a Puritan-Cromwellian simplification to any exuberance and turning was less elaborate. Bun feet of Dutch origin appeared and bobbin turning was used. Leather chairs of Spanish type with brass studding were made.

When Charles II returned to the throne in 1660 he brought Continental craftsmen, particularly Flemish, French and Italians with him. They preferred their familiar walnut to the

2. This type of massive oak table, known as a refectory table from the 19th century onwards, evolved from trestle-supported boards and developed into more sophisticated bulbous-legged and draw tables (tables with secondary leaves under the top, which could be pulled out to extend the length) in the 16th century. This was obviously a table for an important owner and still exhibits the massive construction and carved bulbous legs of earlier times even though it is of c.1620 date. If the frieze is carved or decorated on one side only then the piece was probably a side table.

3. An English joined oak livery table c.1620 with a folding top which could be supported by the back gate leg when open. From it the 'livery', or rations of food and wine, could be distributed to the household. It has a drawer under the top and has column turned supports with an arched frieze between.

4. An English cabinet of c.1630 in which more advanced Renaissance features are remarkably evident, i.e. fluted Ionic pilasters, fluted columns below, scroll and elaborate cartouche carving and a distinct architectural basis to the whole design. It is suggested that this and the right-hand chair in the next illustration are connected with pieces made for Archbishop Laud.

5. Two English oak armchairs of 'wainscot' type, c.1620, the one on the left having strong architectural decoration in the carving of the fluted arched back, the other having a cartouche somewhat related to the cabinet shown in the previous illustration.

6. Bobbin turning and the use of walnut rather than oak came with the Continental influences reaching England after the Restoration in 1660. This side table exhibits the attraction of more sophisticated turning whilst retaining the charm of a provincial or country-made piece.

7. Fully Anglo-Dutch or Flemish in character, this English-made chest of c.1680 shows the ivory, ebony and mother-of-pearl inlays which came to England from the Low Countries (whence they had arrived from Spain) combined with geometric mouldings, arched panels and other features of the Renaissance.

prevailing native oak furniture. A Baroque influence was felt, manifesting itself in the tables with scrolled double-curved legs, spiral or twist turning instead of bobbins, balls or columns, the crown motif, caning of seats and upholstery covered with finer fabrics of all types. Veneering came with foreign craftsmen and marquetry and oystering (parquetry of small branches veneer-cut across the grain) were used. Oriental lacquer furniture came back into fashion. The Italian craftsmen produced gesso, gilded and silvered surfaces.

Items such as bureaux, day beds, sofas, chests of drawers, wing chairs, mirrors, small tables and stands, quite apart from draped four-poster beds, were novelties now produced extensively. Into this period can be included the late Jacobean, brief three year reign of James II.

8. This late 17th century English chest on stand uses 'oysters' – parquetry of small branches veneer-cut across the grain – to achieve its decorative effects, particularly since the wood used, lignum vitae, has a yellow sapwood which emphasises the darker core. The Low Countries influence of the cabinet and the twist turning of the stand show how the arrival of firstly Charles II and then William of Orange to the throne brought Continental craftsmanship to England.

9. The gateleg table made its appearance in the 17th century. The legs could be simply turned, developed into columns, spirals or more elaborate turnings including the bobbins shown on this double-gated example. Usually the tables were made of oak, but elm, ash, walnut, fruitwoods and yew were also used.

With William and Mary the full Baroque splendour came to England. Dutch, Italian and the French influence of Louis XIV's sumptuous court impinged strongly on the work of local craftsmen quite apart from the importation of pieces and skilled practitioners from abroad.

Walnut became the fashionable wood, both veneered and in the solid. Although turned legs continued to be the principal form, the cabriole leg arrived.

Surface treatment included veneering, seaweed marquetry, lacquer and japanning.

1. A joined chest of drawers from Ipswich, Massachusetts, made of red oak painted black, white and red. Dated 1678 and inscribed with initials for John and Margaret Staniford of Ipswich.

AMERICA

In the second half of the century, furniture made in America was taken from English, Flemish and Dutch or German models of the prevailing styles. The English colonies of Puritan New England and the plantations below the Chesapeake Bay are the best known but settlement by the Dutch in the Hudson Valley, Swedes in the Delaware and Pennsylvania 'Dutch' – actually Deutsch, meaning German – in that state, gave rise to separate strains of furniture and decoration based on models brought from the countries of origin. Apart from imported pieces, furniture was very simply made until style and design books were eventually consulted before

construction in oak, pine, ash, elm, poplar, maple and other local woods was undertaken.

In New England there were important centres at Essex County, Massachusetts, north of Boston, and in New Haven, which was absorbed into Connecticut in 1665. Furniture was imported at first but soon local craftsmen started to produce furniture in response to the development of the colony.

Decoration took the form of bulbous turning, split applied turnings and balusters, strapwork, low-relief carving and frequently painted work. The regions of furniture production such as New England, particularly Massachusetts and Connecticut, developed regional styles associated with particular craftsmen who used certain turned, carved or

2 (Left). A chest with drawers under, often known as a mule chest, from Essex County, Massachusetts. Oak and pine painted black and red, with applied split baluster turnings on the front stiles, c.1695.

3 (Below left). A joined press cupboard from Guilford, New Haven, Connecticut, made of red cedar, oak and chestnut, c.1670. This clearly shows its Elizabethan English derivation.

4 (Below). A white and red oak 'wainscot' type chair from Essex County, Massachusetts, c.1680. This form of panelled joined chair, with turned front legs and arm supports, was a common English type. The carving in low relief takes the form of strapwork, scrolls and foliage decoration.

5. A joined press cupboard from Connecticut, made of oak and pine, the details painted black. The decoration takes the form of turned split balusters and moulded surfaces as well as a form of gadrooning under the top moulding and low-relief floral carving to the lower panels. It is suggested that this is similar to other pieces made at Wethersfield, Connecticut Valley.

painted motifs which have assisted in identifying their origin.

Chairs of a variety of types, starting with wainscot English forms and developing into a multiplicity of turned spindle or ladderback versions with wooden or rush seats were made, again using local woods such as ash, hickory, maple or elm. The Brewster and Carver chairs, named after an elder and a governor of the Massachusetts Bay Colony, are examples of so-called 'stick' chairs fashioned after turned or 'thrown' English models.

CHAPTER 4

The 18th Century

GENERAL

In general terms, the eighteenth century produced developments of a relatively coherent type which give a broad guide to assessing pieces and their style or origin. These may be summarised as follows:

1. From the start of the century FRANCE became a very powerful country and exercised enormous influence over the whole period and area in the sense that the latest fashion in France was rapidly translated into other countries. The passing of the century saw the Baroque of Louis XIV change into the curvaceous Rococo of Louis XV, then straighten up into the squarer, straighter outlines of Louis XVI and the Neo-Classical Revival that preceded the severer Empire style of the early nineteenth century. In the illustrations to 'Know Your Louis' (pages 84-87) these features are compared for easy identification. The top quality cabinetmakers – *ébénistes* – were based in Paris even though there were many immigrants among them.

2. England started to become more important and evolved its own, national, distinct styles and standards to the extent that the Low Countries took England as an example of high craftsmanship. The celebrated Chippendale, in 1754, set a pattern for English furniture that was followed by Hepplewhite and Sheraton. All these three published design books that were very influential and were used in Germany, Italy and even France, with whom England was mainly at war.

3. The Oriental influence, which had started much earlier with explorations from the Low Countries, Portugal, France and England, was also felt in many pieces of high fashion. This is dealt with in Chapter 5.

1. A Roman giltwood cradle of the early 18th century which shows how the Italian Baroque was to evolve, as elsewhere, into the scrolling of the Rococo. This flamboyant piece is supported on four scrolls with putti (cherubs) seated on them, shouldering the load, and there are two more above, one holding a garland of flowers. The cradle itself is a carved shell inside which there is an iron swinging basket with a tôle (sheet iron) liner. Additional swags of flowers, acanthus leaves and a shaped, moulded and ebonised base add to the fun.

2. The console table remained an important item of Italian furniture, often with sculptural effects. This Venetian early 18th century example has a Sicilian jasper marble top supported by a rather awkwardly-kneeling (on rocks), unfortunate slave in a flowing robe. The whole thing is on a moulded hexagonal base and scroll feet.

ITALY

At the start of the eighteenth century there was little change from the Baroque styles which had prevailed before. Right through the century there were many houses, both grand and of the increasing bourgeois middle class, which clung to this style. Due to a decline in the trading activities of the country, except perhaps in Venice, wealth was not as lavishly available as it had been and many Italian craftsmen sought employment in France, Germany and England.

The later Baroque styles developed into Rococo, as in France (q.v.), and it is perhaps significant that the still prosperous Venice should be most associated with Rococo in Italy

in this period. The furniture generally reduced from its monumental scale and became more recognisably domestic, with the furnishings of smaller rooms, which were easier to heat in winter, receiving more attention.

Certain pieces of furniture such as chests of drawers, card tables, bureaux and bureau-bookcases, for which England and Holland often provided the models, became popular. By the mid-century the powerful influence of France was having a strong effect and the nearer provinces of Piedmont and Liguria in particular produced furniture of French influence, although the quality of craftsmanship was not as good. Italian versions of Louis XV furniture tended to be exaggerated from the original, with bolder curves and heightened decoration.

3. This mid-18th century Genoese giltwood console table has a verde marble top and an elaborately-scrolled pierced base with mermaids to support it, not to mention a stretcher with cherub and floral and foliate (i.e. leaved) swags.

4. This is a Roman side table of c.1720 with thick marble top and elaborate scroll and leaf decoration to the legs, pierced frieze – which has a female mask at its centre – and X-stretcher. There are grotesque masks on the legs as well.

5. A Venetian Rococo chest of drawers of c.1750 in which the combination of Venetian painted decoration, French Louis XV commode design and idealised landscape scenes are all blended. The top has been simulated to look like marble.

6. In Lombardy the tradition of certosina inlays continued in modified form, here used on a serpentine walnut commode of French inspiration. The inlay is of pewter and ivory in the forms of floral trails, birds and animal heads. There are three long drawers flanked by rounded angles and the piece is raised on carved cabriole legs à la Louis XV. This shape of commode was not only copied from France by the Italians; there were many other national versions, including Chippendale's.

Since pietra dura had become very expensive, the scagliola paste of marble, plaster, isinglass and colouring materials was used in its place and slabs of scagliola were exported to England and other countries for the tops of tables and commodes.

After the mid-century there was a Neo-Classical revival, perhaps due to the popularity of ruins and excavations at Pompeii and Herculaneum. The etchings of

7. This Lombardy walnut chair of c.1750 is again clearly based on French Louis XV designs but exhibits a local, rather stiff and thicker interpretation of the original which nevertheless has a good deal of charm.

9. Earlier forms did not just disappear. This 18th century edition of a Savonarola chair is of carved walnut and has a carved monogram inside a cartouche in the centre of the back.

8. A late 18th century North Italian marquetry commode of Neo-Classical design which is influenced by Louis XVI developments across the Alps. The decoration and the tapering square legs show how fashion had reacted and moved away from the curves of the Rococo.

10. An Italian marquetry bureau of cylinder type, extensively inlaid with peasant scenes, based again on French examples which presaged taste of the 19th century.

11. The Neo-Classical in the Neapolitan manner. A painted and parcel-gilt side table of c.1785 with a mottled pink and white marble top, the frieze carved with leaves and paterae, raised on rather coarse square tapering fluted legs.

Piranesi, which illustrated many famous ruins and classical scenes, may have contributed to this fashion and, since Piranesi was well acquainted with Robert Adam during his time in Italy, this same influence was felt in England. The Neo-Classical revival was also important in France.

Another influence was the taste for versions of the English designers Chippendale, Hepplewhite and Sheraton, whose design books were extant in Italy and from which much furniture was copied.

1. A Boulle three-drawer commode of the Régence period c.1730, in which it can be seen that the Louis XIV outline seen earlier is moving away from stiff squareness to a curvaceous waviness which anticipates Louis XV styles. The art of the metalworker is also very prominent in the effusive applied gilt-metal decoration, which includes the feet, scrolled foliate affairs which have not yet quite got as far as becoming cabrioles. The commode shows the enormous sophistication which French ébénistes could achieve.

2. An early Louis XV kingwood commode of two drawers with marble top, showing a much higher lift of the legs, which end in foliate hoof feet, and still the use of applied bronze decoration of scroll, leaf and other forms in addition to inlaid quartered and crossbanded drawers. Note how the metal mounts sweep out to form handles.

FRANCE

1. Régence 1715-1723

The reign of Louis XIV came to an end in 1715 with the Baroque starting to give way to a softer style. Before the young Louis XV ascended to the throne there was a Regency of Philippe d'Orléans and during this transitional period the strong rectilinear basis of furniture began to be modified into the curves of the forthcoming Louis XV. There was a craze for Chinoiserie due to commercial exploitation in

3. A serpentine Louis XV kingwood bureau plat *(literally a flat bureau, or writing table) which demonstrates the curved cabriole legs with gilt-bronze mounts for which Louis XV is famous. There are three drawers, with decorative gilt-bronze handles and the top is inset with leather and has gilt-bronze borders. The* bureau plat *remained a popular and high-quality piece on into the 19th century and was made in all the prevailing styles.*

the Far East and decoration from porcelain in the form of rocks, shells, flowers and birds was the basis of a manner dubbed 'Rock and Shell' – in French, *Rocaille et Coquille*, from which is taken the word 'Rococo'.

During the Regency the cabriole leg became more common and ornament took natural forms for its inspiration rather than the classical. For this reason ribbons, foliage, shells, and scrolls are the typical language of Rococo decoration. The lighter and more delicate forms affected the use of materials and walnut and ebony began to give way to veneers of lighter woods and polished rosewood.

In this period the commodes of Charles Cressent, with their chased bronze metal ornamentation, are particularly celebrated.

2. Louis XV 1723-1774

The advent of Louis XV to the throne heralded a period which is justly described as one of the greatest in decorative furniture. The prevailing style was the Rococo described above using ornamentation based on shells, flowers, musical instruments, baskets and Chinese themes in marquetry and inlays, which were developed into a high art. The woods used for Louis XV furniture included rosewood, satinwood, amaranth, tulipwood, mahogany, cherry and plum. Painted furniture was also in demand and the colours were very bright – red, green, yellow and black with gilded and other contrasting highlights. Furniture was sent to the Orient to be decorated (see Chapter 6) and local varnishers such as the Martins (*Vernis Martin*) developed local processes in successful competition with this lengthy transportation system.

A great deal of applied metalwork was used in addition to the functional handles, locks and escutcheon plates. This metalwork intended entirely for decorative purposes has met with some disapproval elsewhere but it was generally only used on the most expensive pieces – Meissonier and Caffieri, famous *ébénistes*, were metal workers before producing anything in wood – and most of the

4. A pair of Louis XV walnut fauteuils, c.1750, with moulded frames carved with scrolls and cartouches, the upholstery covered in a needlework fabric with flowers and exotic fruits. Note again the classic cabriole legs. A form of chair that has been made everywhere ever since.

5. A walnut duchesse-brisée, or day bed, formed of three pieces in this case, covered in floral pink silk, again of typical Louis XV shape.

French furniture of the time used metal mounts for functional reasons.

The tops of tables and commodes were of marble or imitations like scagliola (see Italy). Commodes were developed into various other forms, including desks. Console tables were very architectural and a myriad of tables of functional and occasional types were made, all with cabriole legs. A writing table known as a *bureau plat*, basically a longish four-legged table but with all kinds of embellishment, and a favourite of Cressent, came to replace the eight-legged, drawer-pedestalled Bureau Mazarin.

Chairs moved to greater comfort, with low backs to meet fashion requirements. The *bergère* chair, an upholstered winged armchair on short cabriole legs, was made with solid sides and loose cushions (an open-armed chair is called a *fauteuil*) but is not to be confused with the caned English so-called bergère chair

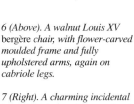

6 (Above). A walnut Louis XV bergère *chair, with flower-carved moulded frame and fully upholstered arms, again on cabriole legs.*

7 (Right). A charming incidental Louis XV piece: a kingwood and tulipwood parquetry table en chiffonière *with trellis parquetry top and gilt-bronze mounts. There is a leather-lined writing slide, two drawers at the side, and a shelf acts as a stretcher between the curving cabriole legs. A highly decorative form of work table for an extremely expensive lady.*

8 (Left). A small bureau in the same manner as the previous piece, showing the decorative nature of the Louis XV style which has kept it a perennial favourite.

9 (Below). Not all Louis XV pieces were exquisite town finery. The French Provincial range of furniture is of enormous attraction. Here is a walnut commode of wavy-fronted (arc-en-arbalette) form, with the scrolls of the Rococo to feet and apron but a plain walnut top (although provincial pieces can have marble tops, too) and pleasant pierced metal handles. c.1750.

of the nineteenth century and after. Caned chairs were also made in this period, usually equipped with loose cushions, and straw or rush-seated chairs were also plentiful.

The chaise-longue is an item much associated with Louis XV perhaps due to the habit of ladies receiving guests whilst reclining upon one. These pieces took the form of an extended chair or a small bed with a headpiece, and a further development was the so-called

10. A Louis XV Provincial walnut armoire (originally an aumbry or press cupboard) a traditional piece which has moved with the times to acquire the Rococo curves of the style but with polished steel mounts instead of gilt-bronze.

duchesse-brisée (broken duchess) which was a day-bed composed of an armchair sometimes with an extra facing armchair with a separate extra section or sections which could be added to it when required.

The great master *ébénistes* of the period were Oeben, Caffieri, Meissonier, Oppenord and Oudry.

11 (Left). At the end of Louis XV's reign, c.1770, style had stiffened and changed to become more upright. This high narrow chest is called a semanier because it has seven drawers, one for each day of the week (semaine = a week, seven days) and is in tulipwood, with a marble top.The short legs are still vaguely cabriole in form, but not as curvy as earlier versions.

12 (Below). Here we have the Louis XVI style in all its straight return to Neo-Classical shaping. This mahogany commode is by the celebrated ébéniste David Roentgen, cabinetmaker to the king, and marks how the reaction away from the Rococo was so strong. This is known as the French Grecian style of c.1785 and its plain surfaces and square tapering legs rely on very restrained decoration of ormolu mounts, drapery swag handles, beaded roundels and beaded edges.

3. The Transitional Style c.1760

Around the middle of the century a reaction to the sinuous scrolls of the Rococo began to set in and furniture tended to stiffen a little, back towards the classical, in preparation for the advent of Louis XVI in the 1770s. Transitional furniture is more restrained than Louis XV and the commode assumed a break-front rather

13. Louis XVI chairs, too, straightened up to become stiff and Classical. These fauteuils exhibit the tapering fluted turned legs typical of the style and the oval (right-hand) or arched (left-hand) padded backs, curved or bow-fronted seats which are also its hallmarks.

than a curved serpentine or bombé frontage or, at least, a curve of less exaggerated form. The cabriole leg is retained in transitional pieces but it has stiffened and straightened to give a lengthier look.

The fine *ébénistes* of the period are Jean-François Oeben, Riesener, Leleu, Oeben's brother Simon and his brother-in-law Vandercruse.

4. Louis XVI 1774-1793

The transitional period led the move away from the Rococo, so that by the time Louis XVI came to the throne, simpler forms and straight lines were back in fashion. There was a return to classicism due to interest in excavations at Pompeii and Herculaneum and this led to the dropping of curves in favour of straight uprights and right-angled joints once again.

In Louis XVI furniture the characteristic straightened leg is turned or tapered and

grooved or fluted. Cabrioles are right out. Bases and capitals come in the form of mouldings or feet. Panels are flat and not highly decorated, with mouldings to emphasise their character. Ornament is in the form of acanthus leaf, egg-and-dart banding, oak leaves, Greek palm leaves, fretwork, ribbons, and so on. Vase turnings, torch effects, bound arrows or fasces, lyres, swans, festoons, urns, wreaths and all the language of Classical, i.e. Greco-Roman, decoration is in. Brass and gilt mouldings emphasised or framed drawers and brass galleries were put round table surfaces, commodes, and bookcases.

The wood was mostly mahogany although tulipwood, rosewood and others could be used. Ebony was back in fashion. Black and gold lacquer and painted furniture in grey, white or pastel greens could be found. Sèvres china plaques were put on to desks and cabinet surfaces. The types of pieces themselves were

14. The fall-front secretaire (secrétaire à abattant) *became popular during this period. This mahogany version c.1785, with white marble top, has the fall down to show the writing surface and the fitted interior with shelves and drawers. The curved canted corners have metal mounts and the piece is raised on bracket feet.*

the same as for Louis XV but changed in style to the Neo-Classical revival. There were a few new shapes such as curule chairs using X-forms and the vitrine for displaying curios.

The great *ébénistes* of this period were Riesener, David (David Roentgen), Jacob et fils, Avril, Carlin, Leleu, Saunier, Lalonde, Aubert and Schwerdfeger amongst others.

15 (Right). A Directoire mahogany table, c.1795, called a guéridon, *with a white marble top and brass inlay to the frieze. The circular undertier is also of white marble. Attributed to Bernard Molitor. Pieces like this, with griffin supports above paw feet and a pierced brass trellis-gallery around the top, have served as examples for copyists ever since. The classical derivation of this furniture – known as 'Etruscan', very popular in Paris – was typical of the last years of the 18th century and of Directoire/Consulate fashion.*

16 (Below). A Directoire chair known as a fauteuil *of c.1790, the structure carved with leaves and painted and parcel-gilded for decoration. The rectangular back and seat are covered in Aubusson tapestry with oval panels (known as reserves) of children and animals, the borders worked with flowers on a blue ground. Note that the top rail of the chair is scrolled over rather than the shaped but upright design of the Louis XVI period.*

5. Directoire 1795-1799
Consulate 1799-1804

After the Revolution the styles were similar to Louis XVI but simpler and the motifs of the Revolution – caps, arrows, spikes, triangles, wreaths, clasped hands, fasces etc – made their appearance on furniture in place of earlier decoration. An 'Etruscan' style was popular in Paris and sabre legs were used on chairs. The top rail of chairs was scrolled over and pierced splats of English type were developed. Jacob was the leading *ébéniste*. Griffins, winged lions, sphinxes and female busts were used as supports. Already hints of the Empire style were coming into furniture construction and design; a transition was taking place.

KNOW YOUR LOUIS – FOURTEEN, FIFTEEN OR SIXTEEN?

These pages have been created so that the essential differences between the three principal Kings of France, each so influential in design terms, can readily be differentiated. The barest essential facts about them are as follows:

1.1. A Louis XIV Bureau Mazarin of c.1690, showing this classic desk form in a marquetry version. Note the strong structural emphasis and square tapering legs, sometimes octagonal or multi-faceted in section.

1.2. A pair of Louis XIV torchères of c.1700 with Boulle metal inlaid decoration. The octagonal tops have raised moulded borders above acanthus leaf capitals on tapering supports. The high scrolled 'Baroque' tripod legs are typical of this date.

Louis XIV (Louis the Fourteenth) 1643-1715

Came to power when his minister Cardinal Mazarin died in 1662. An era of growing power, pomp and baroque splendour for France. Louis XIV furniture is:

- Symmetrical
- Straight-lined
- Dignified

1.3. A Louis XIV commode of king-wood parquetry. At this stage the commode is of bow-fronted design, still rather upright and severe but with some metal mounted decoration. Its structure is simple and most joints are at right angles.

2.1 (Above). This is a typical Louis XV beechwood arm chair, known as a fauteuil. Such chairs can also be gilded or painted. The legs are cabrioles, echoed by the arm supports. The back and frame below the seat are also curved. The pads on the arms and the seat and back are upholstered and covered in floral-patterned textiles, sometimes Aubusson tapestry, as in this case.

2.3 (Above right). Louis XV incidental tables such as this have delightful charm and can take a variety of forms, but nearly always with the slender curving legs seen here and with metal mounts on the leading edges.

Louis XV (Louis the Fifteenth)
1723-1774

Came to power after the Regency (Régence) of Philippe D'Orléans. Rococo became the rage. Louis XV furniture is:

- Asymmetrical – avoids symmetry and right angles as much as possible.
- Curvy, cabriole-legged, scrolled, wavy
- Mounted with gilt metal mounts – ormolu flashes from every corner and surface

2.2. A Louis XV commode. Curves abound everywhere. The metal mounts have spread across the front surface in Rococo scrolls and leaf forms. The serpentine wooden surfaces are covered in marquetry and parquetry of basket-weave form. The legs are cabrioles. Whether in two-drawer or three-drawer versions, Louis XV commodes are always curvaceous.

3.1 (Opposite, top left). A Louis XVI arm chair or fauteuil as a contrast to a Louis XV one. The legs are straight, turned, tapering, even if modestly fluted; the back is square and so is the frame; even the covering is plain.

3.2 (Opposite, below). Before the full Neo-Classical Louis XVI style came into being there was a Transitional Style of the kind seen here, in which the commode has started to straighten up considerably even though the cabriole leg has been retained. This is c.1770. The stepped breakfront form is characteristic of the Transitional Style; it is as though the bulging frontal curves of Louis XV are reluctant to disappear entirely and this central protruberance is the last, flattened echo of bulges of earlier years.

3.3 (Opposite, top right). Another Louis XVI arm chair or fauteuil but this time with an oval back, giltwood frame aand patterned silk upholstery material. Although the effect is lighter than the previous exmple, the structure is still essentially upright and severe, without any of the curves of Louis XV.

3.4 (Above). A Louis XVI commode of c.1780 in which the transition to severe Neo-Classicism has been completed. The front is a straight, flat surface; the cabriole legs have been replaced by tapering turned ones; metal is restricted to handles, keyhole scutcheons and modest corner pieces; the structure is joined at right angles throughout.

Louis XVI (Louis the Sixteenth) 1774-1793

With Louis the Sixteenth the Neo-Classical reaction to Rococo curviness set in. There was a period of transition as the cabrioles straightened up and surfaces flattened, losing their ornamental curviness.

Louis XVI furniture is:

- Square or rectangular again
- On straight turned legs
- Plainer, more severe

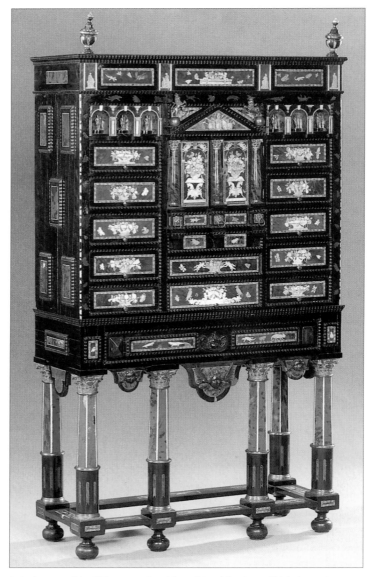

1. At the start of the 18th century Spanish traditional furniture of high decoration, some of it clearly deriving from vargueño *skills like this Hispano-Flemish cabinet, were still being made. Inlays of bone and mother-of-pearl came from Moorish origins even if the motifs were no longer geometric but had moved to flowers, cherubs, birds and other fauna in response to Baroque influences. The stand has been altered at a later date.*

2 (Below). A Spanish walnut centre table with characteristic scrolled iron stretchers and ring-turned legs. This form of table, whether used as an occasional centrepiece, for writing or for eating, was made consistently over a very long period (and still is).

3 (Right). This Neapolitan-Iberian chair of quasi-Louis XVI design, c.1780, illustrates the links between Spain and Naples in the 18th century, since Carlos III had ruled in Naples before his ascent to the Spanish throne. The central splat in the shield-like back is of vase form with surmounting plumes and the overall form is one which, much further North, would perhaps be designated 'French Hepplewhite'.

SPAIN

Philip V (1700-1746)
Ferdinand IV (1746-1759)
Carlos III (1759-1788)
Carlos IV (1788-1808)

The essential influences on Spanish furniture of the eighteenth century are firstly France and later Italy. Philip V was a Bourbon, grandson of Louis XIV, so with him, at the start of the century, French influence is understandable. His two wives were, however, Italian.

Carlos III had ruled in Naples before his ascent to the Spanish throne, so a Neapolitan influence was felt after his arrival.

The effect of these fashions was to produce such items as carved and gilded console tables in the French manner, although the surface treatment was not of the same quality. As in France, the Rococo followed a baroque style

4. A Spanish or Neapolitan rosewood commode in the Louis XVI style of c.1785, of bow-fronted form and the top inlaid with a decoration figuring Leda and the Swan. The basic Neo-classicism of the piece is derived from current French fashion.

and the scrolls and naturalistic forms appear on Spanish furniture in local interpretations. The commode took over from the very Spanish *vargueño*, but Spanish commodes were not as grand as their French parentage and tended to limit their decoration to carved forms of simpler execution on the solid wood. Only in the Royal workshops were grander pieces made for the public rooms of Royal households. Marquetry on Italian lines was produced and it is in eighteenth century Spain that it is possible to find Boulle pieces with Neapolitan marquetry in them.

At the beginning of the century chairs took the form of Louis XIV fauteuils and later there were Louis XV copies. The Portuguese chairs mentioned in the seventeenth century section came further into use and there was also an English influence, particularly for the Queen Anne style, which progressed into George I and Spanish Chippendale chairs as the century wore on.

With the ascent of Carlos IV to the throne the Italian Neapolitan influence was at its strongest, although inevitably the rectilinear Louis XV fashion made itself felt. It was a period in which Spain was a follower of outside influences rather than producing any of its own original designs.

Outside Madrid and fashionable cities, however, traditional furniture continued to be produced.

1. A Portuguese table of Rococo form made from rosewood, mid-18th century, of a type which seems to have been popular. Its serpentine front has two drawers and scroll carving to the frieze. It stands on cabriole legs.

PORTUGAL

John V (1706-1750)
Joseph I (1750-1777)
Maria I (1777-1816)

John V of Portugal was instrumental in bringing Italian and Austrian architects into the country but the agreements between Portugal and England, with whom close ties were established, brought a strong English influence to furniture, which was simpler than the French and Italian models used by Spain.

Chairs in particular were affected by this, with Queen Anne English styles becoming popular, but made in Brazilian woods such as jacaranda and pausanto, whose density and strength

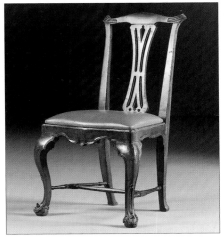

2. A Portuguese walnut dining chair of a design clearly derived from English contemporary chairs of the pre-Chippendale era. Portuguese 'Queen Anne' chairs similarly echoed English-Dutch designs. This chair of c.1750 with its waved top rail, pierced waisted splat, drop-in seat and cabriole legs with scrolled feet is a handsome interpretation of an English design.

3 (Left). A Portuguese
rosewood bureau of c.1755
a sloping fall enclosing
small drawers, pigeonholes
and central cupboard in
the Anglo-Dutch manner
but its serpentine lower
part with four drawers
takes more after French
Provincial styling.

4 (Below). A Portuguese
marquetry commode which
has something of the Louis
XV/Louis XVI Transitional
style in its break front but
is closer to Louis XVI in
severity and straightness of
line. The frieze is inlaid to
imitate fluting and has
three small drawers. The
two long drawers below
are inlaid with ribbon twist
and geometric borders
around quartered false-
panel surfaces.

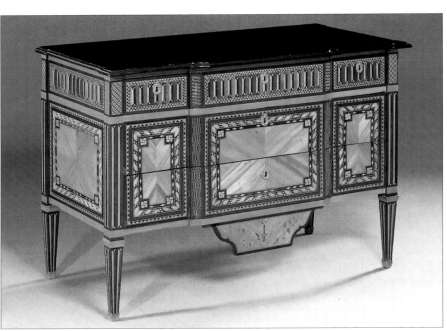

allowed the chairmakers to use thinner sections and crisper lines, without stretchers between legs. In Portugal the cabriole leg stayed popular and Chippendale influences did not seem to extend themselves to the square 'Chippendale' leg. The cabriole remained in use.

There was use of Baroque styles, passing on to Rococo Chippendale, and towards the end of the century the English influence was even more marked. Commodes in the French style were produced, however (as they were in England), again sometimes using different woods from the originals. Other English pieces such as gateleg tables, pie-crust tripods and incidental furniture were made by Portuguese craftsmen who had access to imported models and design books.

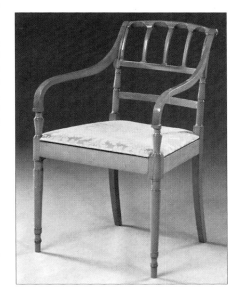

5 (Above). A Portuguese walnut and parcel-gilt commode of c.1750, clearly taking Louis XV French influences for its inspiration, but with rather exaggerated bombé curves and gilt Rococo scrolling. A high quality interpretation of a fashionable trend.

6 (Right). This satinwood Portuguese chair with down-curved arms, arcaded back and slender turned legs could easily be mistaken for an English chair of similar date, say 1790. The seat is in fact caned, with a loose cushion on it.

1. The classic Dutch shape – a mahogany bureau bookcase shown fully open, with pedimented top, moulded panelled doors enclosing stationery compartments, drawers and pillared central cupboard, a sloping fall front inset with leather writing surface and enclosing further drawers and stationery compartments, and three long drawers in the bombé-shaped lower section, raised on cabriole legs with ball and claw feet. c.1750.

THE LOW COUNTRIES

At the Revocation of the Edict of Nantes in 1685 large numbers of Huguenot craftsmen fled from France to England and to the Low Countries. Their influence was strongly felt in terms of the sophistication of their furniture styles but it became modified as the ties between England and Holland strengthened with William III on the English throne at the turn of the century.

It is thus usual to find cabriole-legged chairs

2 *(Below, left). This Dutch walnut stool of c.1720 shows the scrolling of the Rococo as it emerged from Baroque styles. The seat is of quatrefoil (four-leafed) shape and the scrolled stretchers of X-form are capped by a finial at the central cross-point. The scrolled legs are carved with acanthus leaves and have a bobbin-turned section just under the seat frame.*

3 *(Right). A Dutch marquetry chest of c.1740, with a double-serpentine front not dissimilar to the French provincial* arc-en-arbalette *shape of the chest in that section. This form of marquetry, on a rosewood ground in this case, with birds, flowers and urns, became a Dutch speciality.*

4 *(Right). A Dutch marquetry chair of c.1740 with an inlaid panel depicting Mercury in the baluster-shaped splat. This wavy form of chair is very akin to English Queen Anne chairs which were derived from the Dutch influence of William III, but the English generally developed a more restrained version. The exuberance of Dutch chairs is usually their distinguishing characteristic but there were very close parallels to English and to Portuguese chairs of the same period.*

5. A Dutch marquetry bureau bookcase which repeats much of the shaping of example 1 but of wider, lavishly embellished surfaces on which the marquetry craftsman has done his utmost to impress the viewer. Urns and flowers are contained within every available panel, whether flat or curved. Such marquetry was made on well into the 19th century and still is.

6. The Dutch love of china and Delftware led to enormous numbers of display cabinets of this type being produced, mainly in walnut but also of marquetry and in mahogany and other woods such as plain oak. The shape is the almost compulsory one incorporating an arched moulded cornice above a glazed pair of doors, canted sides, a shaped lower section with drawers and, in this case, the whole smothered with floral marquetry on a walnut ground.

of Dutch 'Queen Anne' characteristics being produced in the first quarter of the century, although the Dutch versions tend to be more curvaceous and extravagant than the English versions and often used the floral marquetry for which Holland had become famous.

Another piece which might be thought of as typically 'English' is the double-dome walnut bureau-bookcase, which Dutch craftsmen took to with avidity and modified into a recognisably Dutch form, much less rectilinear and with flowing curves not seen in the English

version. Again, marquetry was often used by Dutch craftsmen and corners might be chamfered and the drawer fronts block-moulded or even serpentine in bombé form.

By the mid-eighteenth century the Rococo had made itself felt in the Low Countries and bombé commodes of French inspiration were being made in considerable numbers, moving on to the more severe lines of Louis XVI in the last quarter of the century. The large glazed cabinets popular for the display of china wares continued in production.

GERMANY

At the start of the eighteenth century Germany was still divided in a series of princedoms and individual trading cities. There was, as before, a distinct difference between North and South, with different influences, French-Italian to the South and Anglo-Dutch to the North, intermingling with each other.

The Baroque style which was prevalent at the start gave way slowly and the Régence style, with Boulle inlays, intarsia, bombé commodes and all the trappings of French origin became fashionable. This produced a type of hefty parquetry burgher furniture in Southern Germany which is fairly characteristic.

The Rococo of Louis XV came to Bavaria via Lorraine. The same motifs – birds, fruit, flowers, musical instruments and even garden tools – were used on the consoles, mirror frames, grand chairs and cabinet furniture made by German masters of the time. The style

spread to the Northern palaces even though there was still much importation of pieces from France. German Rococo, however, has a solid

1 (Above). A walnut Frankfurt Wellenschrank, or armoire, of the early 18th century, which shows the heavier Low Countries influence. The use of walnut and the emphasis on the figure and quality of the wood is significant; the moulded panelled doors and the cross-grained mouldings of cornice and base have no ebonising, which would have been the case in the 17th century. It is possible that the piece may originally have been mounted on a stand; the bun feet are later replacements.

2 (Right). By contrast this South German armoire of c.1720 is all parquetry, inlaid strapwork, carved capitals to the Corinthian pilasters and a much lighter approach than the Frankfurt Wellenschrank.

3. (Left) A Dresden walnut bureau cabinet of a type which could be found in England and Holland at the same period, c.1720. The upper section, with its gilded cresting and plumed bust, is perhaps a little grander in decoration than most English bureaux cabinets of this type would display, but the canted corner Corinthian pilasters and simple mirrored door are very similar. The lower half, with its sloping fall above three small, two short, and two long drawers, on ogee bracket feet, could easily be English or Dutch.

4. (Opposite) A South German walnut and parquetry display cabinet c.1745 which has typical features in the serpentine base of three drawers, the basket-weave parquetry inlays and the trelliswork pilasters and scrolled cornice to the top.

quality not seen in French work and there are regional variations which require detailed study in order to get a grasp of the overall picture of the time.

The Frankfurt and Hamburg cupboards of seventeenth century creation gradually changed in style towards the middle of the century, losing some of the heavier architectural features such as columns and cornices in favour of lighter decoration and the broken pediment. Chairs moved towards English and Dutch examples with cabriole legs although later German cabrioles tend to have a more pronounced 'knee' than English or Dutch types.

5. This yew-wood German coiffeuse, or dressing table, of c.1760 shows distinct French influence in the cabriole legs and the serpentine curves of the drawer fronts.

With the advent of Neo-classicism in Louis XV's France, German furniture from the 1770s follows this path and straightens up into the more severe style. One famous cabinetmaker, David Roentgen, spent much time in Paris as the king's *ébéniste* and made German Neo-

6. A grand German Rococo walnut bureau cabinet possibly from Mainz, near Frankfurt, c.1765, on which the decorative features include parquetry, carved pilasters, cartouches, Corinthian capitals, free-standing attached scrolls, lozenges, foliage, flowers and waves.
The lower section is of serpentine form and, although it is an impressive piece, it seems the maker has imposed as many curves as possible on what is essentially a square-rectangular carcase for the purpose for which it was intended.

Classical furniture of high skill and finish for his grander clients. English influence from Hepplewhite and Sheraton began to make itself felt at the end of the eighteenth century and then the Empire style of Napoleonic France led to a local modification of lighter form, dubbed Biedermeier, which belongs to the nineteenth century.

7. Another product of Dresden, but this time in the Louis XV mode, c.1760. This walnut parquetry commode of serpentine bombé shape, with inlaid strapwork and scrolling curves to sides and apron, follows French examples in a local interpretation.

8. Not all furniture followed immediate fashion. A heavy German walnut kas or armoire of the 18th century on which the earlier traditions of heavy Baroque furniture, particularly the spiral columns, can be seen. There are lozenge panels, inlaid lines, scroll corbels and all the paraphernalia of much earlier forms.

9. This German Neo-Classical walnut commode of c.1790 with brass mountings is clearly of French Louis XVI interpretation but in this case of strong architectural character.

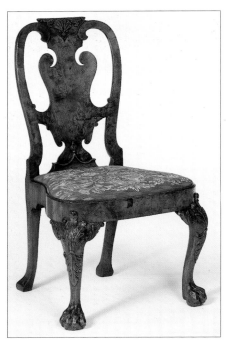

1. An English walnut cabriole-legged chair with a developed fiddle-shaped splat, the drop-in seat covered with needlework. The date is c.1720 and therefore technically George I, although 'Queen Anne' would be the description many would use. The legs have stylised shell carving on the knee and hairy paw feet.

ENGLAND

1. Queen Anne (1702-1714)

The start of the eighteenth century in England sees the continuation of the Dutch influence of the William and Mary-William III version of Louis XIV Baroque furniture. The cabriole leg became much more fashionable. There was a particularly English restraint in the curves of the flowing Baroque outlines and a national style began to emerge. Marquetry was not considered as important as the line of the piece and the fine walnut surfaces which were the fashion. Although carving was used in the form of the scallop shell, scrolls and acanthus leaves, it too was restrained.

New furniture for tea drinking brought forth many small tables. China cabinets, secretaries, bookcases, mirrors, chests-on-chests or chests-on-stands, fire screens and other new pieces were made. The Queen Anne style, mostly

2. A veneered walnut chest on chest (or tallboy, in America) of c.1720 (George I) with fluted canted corners. Three short drawers above three long ones in the top half and three long drawers in the lower half. This form of chest on chest was also made on into the mahogany period and could have extras such as brushing or writing slides, a secretaire drawer, and possibly a 'sunburst' inlaid and inset into the bottom drawer.

associated with the cabriole leg, the double-dome bureau bookcase, the 'fiddle-back' splat in the wavy walnut chair, and the 'Dutch' gable in the cornice, in reality very often the style of the early part of George I's reign, has remained popular ever since.

2. Early Georgian (1714-1760)

Although much of the furniture of the early part of the reign of the Hanoverian kings is difficult to distinguish stylistically from Queen Anne, there was after 1720 or so a move towards the heavier aspects of the Baroque in the grand furniture made for grand houses, which were built in the Italian Baroque style. This took the form of fluted or reeded pilasters, great pediments and architectural features of the kind associated with William Kent. The Rococo development of the Baroque soon modified this ponderousness and cabrioles ended in ball and claw feet or hoof feet, lion masks were used and scrolls, rock-and-shell, satyrs and naturalistic

3. A walnut wing armchair of George II period, c.1750, showing how the cabriole leg with shell carving survived into what is essentially the mahogany era. The form goes back much earlier to Queen Anne times.

4. A mahogany lowboy with a moulded top and one long drawer above three short ones, on cabriole legs, c.1740. A form of table associated with Queen Anne furniture but which remained popular long after.

5 (Above left). The bureau of the late 17th and the 18th century has remained a popular piece of furniture. This walnut example of c.1725 is a typical example of provincial furniture, eminently practical, which was subsequently made in mahogany on into the 19th century.

6 (Above right). An English 'red walnut', i.e. solid American walnut, chair of c.1740 with cabriole legs but the back now flaring out at the top corners in a 'pre-Chippendale' shape heralding things to come. The pierced vase-shaped splat has scroll and leaf carving. The feet are shaped in what is called trefoil form. Compare this with a similar chair in the Portuguese section (page 91).

7 (Right). A mahogany games table of c.1745 with its shaped top open to show the baize lining, the circular corner candlestands and scoops for counters. The cabriole legs are carved with acanthus leaves and have ball and claw feet.

8. In England in the 1740s there was a Classical movement led by architectural designers such as William Kent who designed grand mahogany pedimented furniture such as this bookcase in the Palladian style, with a broken pediment above centred by a cartouche, octagonal-pane glazed doors above four fielded cupboards on a plinth base. Much English Georgian furniture embodies these characteristics.

forms made their appearance.

Walnut, which was the leading wood from roughly 1685 until about 1725-30, began to give way to mahogany and the terms 'Walnut Period' and 'Mahogany Period' have been used to distinguish furniture from these eras as an alternative to the name of a monarch. The removal of import taxes on mahogany in 1733

9 (Above). A serpentine mahogany chest of c.1760 which is English but has borrowed just a little from French commodes. The top has a gadrooned edge and the canted corners are stop-fluted. The bracket feet are panelled and there is a brushing slide beneath the top and above the first of the four long serpentine-fronted drawers.

10 (Left). Although many Chippendale-designed chairs had cabriole legs, it is perhaps with the restrained square straight leg that he is most associated. This fine chair of c.1765 exhibits elements of both the Gothic and the Rococo in the leaf carving and piercing of the splat. The deceptive legs, chamfered from the square at the inside edge, have blind-fret carving, curved corner brackets and matching pierced-fret H stretchers.

11 (Opposite). The tripod table was one of the many receiving stylistic attention in the 18th century. This mahogany version of c.1755 has a hinged galleried top mounted on a four-pillar 'birdcage' enabling it to tip up and rotate, in turn, on a spirally fluted baluster column and three leaf-carved cabriole legs ending in ball and claw feet.

made it much more economic to use and since it is a harder, crisper and more durable material it soon overtook walnut as the first wood for fine and utilitarian furniture.

3. Later Georgian (1760-1811)

In the 1750s and onwards there were several major developments which affected the style of English furniture profoundly. These were:

Chippendale
The publication of Thomas Chippendale's *The Gentleman and Cabinet Makers' Director* (known as the *Director*) in 1754 has provided a useful name to describe mid-Georgian furniture. There were similar publications by the Langleys, Swan, Jones, Lock, Johnson and others but Chippendale confined himself to

furniture and showed almost every type of the time, including, Rococo, Chinese, Gothic and so on. The book was an enormous success and set the pattern for English furniture. One of the strengths of the designs is in their sense of structure, so that whatever the ornament being used, the proportion and scale of the basic piece is maintained. There have been many copyists of Chippendale, who did not make a great deal of furniture himself, some of them producing quite distinctive work of recognisably valid and individual variation such as Irish Chippendale and Philadelphia Chippendale, and many others of less merit.

Adam
The brothers Robert and James Adam were architects who employed cabinetmakers to

12. The shield-back Hepplewhite chair, along with the camel-back, has been a perennial favourite. This mahogany example is in fact a 19th century reproduction but is of high quality and faithful to the original except for the slight baluster swelling to the fluted front legs.

14. Sheraton designed many pieces of furniture, mostly with square tapering legs. This arm chair of c.1780 has three interlaced vertical splats to the back and falls within the 'Sheraton' nomenclature of this square late 18th and early 19th century style.

13. The pedestal desk of Georgian design is also a perennial favourite. This mahogany example of c.1770 is a 'partners' desk', i.e. with identical fittings on both sides so that it can stand in the centre of a room. Such desks, mostly in lesser forms and in other woods, have been made ever since.

15. The Age of Satinwood saw 'Adam' design features return to favour, especially the ribbons, swags and medallions taken from Classical examples. This demi-lune (half moon) or half-round commode of c.1775 is an example of the highest quality fine craftsmanship associated with the style.

execute their designs. Robert had spent time in Italy and was fascinated by the excavations at Herculaneum. When he set up in London in 1758 he brought the Classical influence which was to affect France but not in Louis XV form; the Adam form was more direct and more delicate. It went in for straight lines rather than curves, used motifs such as swags, festoons, rinceaux (a continuous spiral or wavy form), Greek keys, honeysuckle and mythological figures, rams' heads, lions' heads, centaurs, griffins, sphinxes, caryatids and all the paraphernalia associated with Classicism. It was very formal and perhaps a little cold. Its logical outcome was the Satinwood Period and painted decoration is also typical of Adam.

Hepplewhite

The earlier Hepplewhite designs show a French Rococo influence but his most important work is not as curvilinear or scrolled. His chairs are perhaps the things he is best known for, and these tend to have straight tapering legs with backs in one of five variants: the shield, wheel, oval, camel and

heart. The three feathers of the Prince of Wales' crest is a typical motif but so are ribbons, wheat, swags, paterae (small oval or round carved decorations) and so on.

Some of his pieces are painted like Adam's. He also designed chests, commodes, sideboards and desks as well.

Sheraton

Sheraton was a designer and publisher of several books from 1791 onwards. He is thought to have covered the whole gamut of contemporary styles. His earliest work is like Louis XVI, i.e. rectilinear and Neo-classical, with some inlay and porcelain plaques for decoration. He liked ingenious pieces with mechanical contrivances. His work illustrates many pieces of furniture of a wide variety of purposes but the examples of his later publications, confused by French Directoire and Empire models, tend to be over-ornamental. This is a pity because his earlier work shows great understanding of construction, like Chippendale, and has served as a model for many imitators and reproducers ever since.

16. The gateleg table, which made its appearance in the 17th century (see Chapter 3) continued to be made in country woods such as oak and elm in traditional forms throughout the 18th century. With the taste for mahogany, however, more sophisticated designs were needed and these examples show how the cabriole leg was used on mid-18th century mahogany gateleg dining tables.

17 (Right). The gateleg table had limitations in the space available below the top surface. Dining tables of late Georgian style relied on pedestal or pillar supports to allow greater clearance for the sitters. They came in multiple pedestals for longer tables; a single pedestal type is often referred to as a breakfast table – see Chapter 6 on the 19th century. This multi-pedestal mahogany table, shown with three pedestals, has reeded edges to the top, which is mounted on turned column supports with triple legs at the ends and quadruple legs in the centre.

18. *In the early 18th century the country chair makers of the beech woods around Windsor produced a chair which has become known as the Windsor chair. This version of c.1750 shows the early comb-back version (see the 19th century for a hoop-back) in sophisticated form, with cabriole legs rather than turned legs, a vase-shaped splat of 'Queen Anne' origins and dished elm seat. The chair was made for garden use, painted black or green, but rapidly became so very popular that it was used in dozens of other circumstances. It spread to America, where it was made from 1725 onwards in distinct American forms.*

19. *Another vernacular piece of furniture which has remained perennially popular is the country dresser which became steadily universal as a piece of kitchen furniture from mid-century onwards. The word dresser is derived from a side table on which food was 'dressed, i.e. prepared, before being set out for eating. This early yew wood and cherrywood dresser shows a classic form with shelves above.*

The 18th century in England can thus be summarised as follows:

Walnut Period – Queen Anne and Early Georgian
Curved, cabriole-legged furniture of Dutch and Baroque inspiration developing into the first identifiable English styles.

Mahogany Period – Early and Late Georgian
Baroque-Rococo until about 1755, with solid proportion, robust decoration and ornament, shown in Chippendale's earlier work.

Classical Revival
Going from Adam onwards into finer, straighter, slimmer, even spindlier pieces until the Satinwood Period is reached in the early nineteenth century.

1. A fine classical brass-mounted carved mahogany sideboard, New York, c.1815, the rectangular top with scrolled splashboard surmounted by pineapple finials and flanked by a brass gallery, the case below with three drawers above a pair of hinged cupboard doors, the arched centre section with carved Prince of Wales feather centering fluted and carved Ionic half-columns, the reeded base on frontal carved animal paw feet.

AMERICA

There were certain separate and parallel developments in American furniture which followed the lines of the various settlements.

In the early eighteenth century New England furniture was of a simple panelled construction with elementary decorative treatment tailored partly to the available materials and skills and partly to Puritan instincts. English seventeenth century furniture provided the models from which local adaptations were taken.

In Virginia and the Southern plantation colonies, however, there was less religion and more money. Even as far back as 1653 a Virginian colonist could send to Savile Row for his latest suit of clothes. The decoration was more elaborate and imports provided a greater source of pieces than in the New England states.

The Pennsylvanian Germans made pieces with Middle European painted decoration of peasant type and the Swedish and Dutch settlements of the Delaware and Hudson respectively started to make furniture of a simple nature in their own national traditions. Although furniture made in the more frontier

2 *(Above). The Windsor chair was made in America from 1725 onwards, starting in Philadelphia. As in England, the comb-back was the first type, becoming supplanted by the stronger hoop-back by the end of the century. American Windsor chairs soon developed their own particular characteristics: they omitted the heavy English central splat to the back but had thicker seats and legs often raked at a more extreme angle.*

3 *(Right). A walnut 'Queen Anne' highboy of c.1760 of New England type which follows English and Dutch designs of the period.*

areas was of necessity fairly primitive, the European influences along the Eastern coast ensured that some of the latest Baroque designs or their English, French and Flemish variants could be expected to appear within a reasonably short time of their inception. The use of walnut, so universal in Louis XIV and Italian furniture of the late seventeenth century, could be echoed in America by the use of the dark native *juglans nigra* or black walnut, and the turnings, carvings and cabriole legs of eighteenth century Europe were soon in evidence amongst American furniture makers.

The pieces being made soon came to be the recognisable standards of Early American furniture sophistication: highboys or chests-on-stands, lowboys or cabriole-legged three-drawer side tables, chests, upholstered chairs

4 (Left). An early 18th century American walnut small table often known as a 'tavern' table with a circular top set on four turned legs joined by square stretchers.

5 (Below). The gateleg table of English type was made in local American woods. This example is early 18th century.

6 (Bottom). Pennsylvania Germans produced characteristic painted furniture with peasant motifs such as flowers and urns. The tulip – a symbol of Dutch exoticism – was also a favourite form. This chest decoration dates from 1803 but follows earlier motifs.

7 (Right). The 'Queen Anne' American highboy of c.1740-60 is noted for its cabriole legs and shell or 'rising sun' decoration. The broken pediment at the top reflects the architectural influence of William Kent and his followers in England.

8 (Above). Another American favourite of 1740-60 is the lowboy, again made in local woods and tending to be deeper than the equivalent English version. Shell carved decoration is also characteristic.

and so on. The block front chest and bureau, with shell-carved decoration of the Rococo and often associated with Newport, Rhode Island, has been perennially associated with America, although it was a Dutch and English form, also reproduced in the Far East for the European market.

Mahogany was soon identified, as in Europe, as a harder, crisper wood and replaced walnut in many types of sophisticated furniture, although local woods such as maple, cherry and pine continued to be the source of local country craftsmen. Cabinetmakers in

Boston, Newport, New York, and Philadelphia, which was an important centre, began to develop a high degree of skill. Much of their work was of Georgian English inspiration although there were other influences and trade with China (in which Salem specialised) brought an Oriental influence examined in Chapter 6. The American Chippendale style of 1760 to 1780 was particularly rooted in Philadelphia, where the Queen Anne style had predominated, especially for walnut chairs.

Although the Windsor chair was brought to America from England (the first recorded

9. The blockfront kneehole dressing table and blockfront bureau are much associated with Newport, Rhode Island, although versions did arrive from Holland, England and the Far East (see Chapter 6). Made in the solid, of walnut, mahogany and other woods, they are very desirable. This example has prominent cabriole legs.

reference to a Windsor chair is that in the will of a Philadelphia merchant in 1708), the fabrication of Windsor chairs started in America in 1725 and soon quite distinct American Windsors were developed using local woods and lighter, springier designs to the backs, usually without the heavier English splat, but thicker seats and legs at a more raked angle. As in England these chairs were usually painted green or black and were made outsside (rather than in a workshop). By the end of the century the New England Windsor was a distinct type, often with imitation bamboo

10. An American walnut side chair of Philadelphia make in the 'Chippendale' manner, c.1775. It has Gothic tracery in the splat and the cabriole legs end in ball and claw feet. A faithful version of an English type.

11. American cherrywood tables from Connecticut show great charm in the use of cabriole legs and shaped friezes. This example of c.1750 is delightful, using characteristic English pad feet.

12 (Left). A walnut 'bonnet top' chest on chest of c.1770, New England, with broken pediment and shell carved decoration, on bracket feet.

13 (Above). An American maple bureau (or slant top desk) of c.1770, showing a characteristic English/ Dutch form of fairly plain execution on bracket feet. The decorative brass handles and scutcheons are sometimes known as willow plates in America.

14. A simple American Windsor settee of late 18th century date, made by Letchworth of Philadelphia. Note the ringed 'bamboo' turning of the legs. Philadelphia Windsor chair makers exported their products extensively, to many countries including England.

15. A simple American walnut mule or blanket chest on serpentine bracket feet, Pennsylvania c.1770. The lid lifts to provide storage space above the two lower drawers.

16. An American walnut sideboard, possibly Virginia, c.1790. Although from the 'Federal' period it is again based on an English model of pleasing simplicity.

turning and cream or yellow paint, which was exported from Boston as were Pennsylvania Windsors from Philadelphia in large numbers.

Other forms of country chair such as ladderbacks were also made prolifically and the rocking chair, more popular than in Europe, was made in forms that are uniquely American.

After the Declaration of Independence a period known as the Federal Period came into

18. High chest of drawers, maple and pine, north eastern New England, 1740-1765. The original decoration of fanciful burls is black on dark ochre.

17. Federal period secretaire bookcase of c.1810, from Eastern Massachusetts. It is of a design associated with Sheraton but derived from French Directoire furniture.

fashion with an aversion to English styles and promotion of French and Italian models. This return to classicism, which followed the straight lines of Louis XVI and the Directoire, eventually brought about furniture of what might be called Sheraton-Directoire style, one particularly associated with the celebrated Duncan Phyfe (of New York) furniture; it is in fact hard to separate from similar English pieces, which themselves had taken a leaf from France's books quite apart from the classicism of Adam, who also influenced American makers until the Revolution.

CHAPTER 5

The Oriental Influence

The expeditions of the Dutch, English and French trading companies to India and the Far East in the seventeenth century caused a tremendous interest in Oriental artefacts in addition to the spices, silks, tea and other items which were being traded. In addition to this, Venetian, Portuguese and Spanish navigation and colonisation had been involved in exploration to the Near and Far East even longer, returning with porcelain and lacquer work which stimulated demand.

In Europe the craze for Chinoiserie, Japanning and similar decoration started therefore in the seventeenth century but went on unabated throughout the eighteenth, bringing America into its orbit, and continued well into the nineteenth century. It is said that because high quality woods were difficult to obtain in Venice, painted decoration on rough pine cabinet work became the norm and by the end of the seventeenth century much of this Venetian work was in the Oriental taste.

The forms of decoration were not always well defined or understood by European cabinet-makers and decorators, however. Designs from the Middle East such as Persia were mixed up with China, Japan and India, so that pagodas, foliage, Chinese figures, landscapes, monkeys and exotic birds could all occur on one piece. In England the work was often referred to as Coromandel, although this is on the Indian coast, because the ships of the East India Company,

1. A 'Batavian' domed chest on stand, late 17th/early 18th century, showing black lacquer with gilt birds, butterflies and flowers as decoration. In England, incised lacquer was sometimes referred to as 'Bantam' work, hailing from a province of Java called Bantam where in 1603 the English had established a factory and trading post for pepper and Chinese goods, from which they were ejected by the Dutch in 1682. The name Batavia in Java, used by the Dutch, comes from an ancient province between the Rhine and the Waal. The stand is carved with Baroque scrolling foliage and masks and is raised on cabriole legs ending in ball and claw feet.

2 (Below). A 'Coromandel' lacquer chest on stand with long doors decorated with Chinoiserie figures and pagodas. The term Coromandel was mistakenly used in England for Oriental work (Coromandel is on the coast of India) because of the association with the East India Company who traded between India and China. The stand, of 17th century Baroque form with putti, mermaids, dolphins etc., etc., would have been made in England to support a cabinet made up from panels brought from the Orient.

3 (Right). A German lacquer cabinet on stand of c.1710, possibly made in Berlin by Dagly, showing Oriental figures, flowers, foliage, birds and pagodas. Dagly produced such work for Frederick I, who was a keen collector of Oriental work including porcelain.

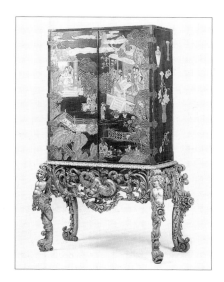

who traded from India to China to pick up tea, were often those bringing the pieces home.

The Oriental trade rapidly became a two-way affair. At first, pieces such as lacquer panels were imported and built into locally-made frames or carcase work. Cabinets were made up from panels and put on a stand of the latest fashion – Baroque or Rococo – built locally in Europe. Then pine or deal carcases, tables and other pieces were made in Europe, shipped to the Far East and lacquered or decorated by Far Eastern craftsmen and returned for sale. This was expensive, so European craftsmen such as the Martin brothers in France, famous for *Vernis Martin* , rapidly learned the art of Japanning or lacquering, as it was called, and produced it locally. In Germany lacquer furniture is associated with Gérard Dagly (from Spa, in the Low Countries) in Berlin, who made copies of

4. A cabinet on stand of late 17th/early 18th century date, the stand of Japanese takamakie *lacquer decorated with gilt scenes, the stand English, 'japanned' with black and gold decoration and leaf-carved feet.*

5. A late 17th century cabinet on chest of drawers, lacquered in gilt on a black ground and decorated with wildlife, mainly birds, figures and pavilions. Inside the brass-mounted cabinet is an arrangement of drawers, also similarly decorated. The chest of drawers is of late 17th century English William and Mary style and may have been made locally to fit the cabinet.

6 (Left). A Dutch display cabinet of the classic shape c.1700 but decorated with black and gilt Chinoiserie figures, buildings and foliage. This may have been done in the Orient or by Dutch craftsmen imitating imported Oriental work.

7 (Opposite). An Iberian lacquer cabinet of c.1730 with sloping lid, decorated with gilt, red and cream Turquerie *figures, foliage and buildings, not Chinese, on a black ground. Inside there are drawers and the stand is on cabriole legs with ball and claw feet.* Turquerie *was an alternative to Chinoiserie in the desire to depict travel in distant countries and was used by French* ébénistes *as well, but the method of lacquering is the same.*

Oriental work from 1687 onwards for Frederick I and with Dresden, where an apprentice of Dagly's called Schnell did similar work for Augustus II. In America in the eighteenth century, japanned furniture was produced in Boston and Philadelphia amongst other centres, and there was importation of Oriental-made pieces probably via England, but more furniture came directly from the early nineteenth century onwards as, after the Revolution, direct trade between China and America increased, especially involving the port of Salem.

In Portugal the same pattern of development from the late seventeenth century onwards can be traced, with Oriental lacquer pieces with red, black and green grounds, particularly cupboards but also chairs in 'Queen Anne' or early eighteenth century English styles, being produced. Portugal also had a strong Indo-Portuguese connection via Goa, and Brazilian sources, which require a separate examination in terms of their style, decoration and place in the evolution of Portuguese furniture.

During the eighteenth century, however, the Far Eastern craftsmen were not slow to realise that they could profit from the burgeoning European and American market for European forms of furniture copied from models or designs brought to them by enterprising traders.

8. An Oriental-made Chinese lacquer chair using Asian woods c.1730 but made for the English market in an early Georgian cabriole-legged style. In all other respects the piece is identical to any Queen Anne/George I chair.

9. An English red and gilt japanned double dome bureau bookcase of early 18th century style, decorated with Chinoiserie figures and landscapes. This Anglo-Dutch form is also to be found in Dresden work of the same period and has been reproduced and imitated since.

10. A Portuguese red parcel-gilt chair of c.1740 in an early Georgian English style, with the baluster shaped splat decorated with a Chinoiserie figure. The caned seat is serpentine fronted and the cabriole legs, on ball and claw feet, are decorated with shells. This form of chair was made in Portugal in large numbers and Chinoiserie was also popular as in other European countries.

11. A French Louis XV commode in black and gold lacquer with ormolu mounts c.1750. The top is of a type known as brêche d'Alèp *marble and there are two long drawers decorated with a Chinese water land-scape with a pagoda and attendants at a tea ceremony. The piece is attributed to Leonard Boudin, who was noted for sunburst marquetry but who also did Chinese lacquer work.*

12. A Venetian table of mid-18th century date, with chamfered top and shaped apron on cabriole legs, decorated with musicians, Chinoiserie figures, pagodas, trees and landscapes. The carved and painted finial on the X-stretcher is a blackamoor musician.

They therefore made European and American style pieces which were faithful copies even if frequently executed in local exotic woods such as padouk and rosewood.

The trade therefore developed rapidly throughout the eighteenth century and by the

13 (Left). A block-front bureau in padouk or rosewood of c.1750, made in the Far East for the English or Dutch market and subsequently shipped to America. The craftsmen of the Far East were quick to realise the potential of the growing European market for furniture in the 18th century.

14. (Below). A Venetian commode of mid-18th century date with Chinoiserie scenes in blue on a creamy yellow ground within parcel-gilt borders. Venice had traded with the Near and Middle East before the Dutch, English and French trading companies of the 17th century were set up and had a tradition of painted furniture due to shortages of fine woods.

nineteenth century had become a brisk industry. There were several variations, viz.

- Initially, Oriental panels brought to Europe and built into furniture by European cabinetmakers
- Carcase work made in Europe, shipped out to the Far East, lacquered and decorated with Oriental scenes, then returned for sale
- Pieces made entirely in the Orient
- Pieces made entirely in Europe and, eventually, in America
- Oriental or colonially-made furniture copied in the latest European fashion and shipped to Europe or America. Some pieces in local exotic woods and some more conventionally in mahogany.

15. (Right) A French green lacquer secretaire à abattant, or fall-front secretaire desk of mid- to later 18th century form with ormolu mounts, the fall decorated with a lakeside Chinoiserie vista and the lower cupboard doors painted with floral sprays, the sides similarly decorated.

16 (Below right). An English Regency japanned chair of c.1810 with gilt Chinoiserie decoration and 'bamboo' frame. There was a strong vogue for Chinese decoration in this period, the fashion led by the Prince Regent in particular, with the Brighton Pavilion eventually providing an extreme example.

17 (Below). A 'Sheraton' metamorphic dressing table made from Oriental hardwoods with brass fittings and castors, c.1800. Sheraton was fond of this type of multi-purpose furniture and there are several examples in his design books, such as his 'Harlequin' table. This must have been an ideal piece to copy for Oriental use or for shipping back to England for sale. The functions of washing, dressing, writing and even eating can be satisfied by this piece.

127

18. In the 19th century the sewing table enjoyed great popularity and was produced in many forms. This black and gilt lacquer example of c.1835 decorated with a view of Macao was made for the Wetmore family of Newport, Rhode Island.

The effect of the craze for Chinoiserie in the late seventeenth century was to influence design with its more decorative, pictorial and fantasy approach, so that the vogue for Rococo is said to have been inspired by this craze. Eventually the return to Classicism at the end of the eighteenth century abated this decorative trend in favour of severity, but revivals broke out from time to time, notably in Regency England of the early nineteenth century and on to the present day.

CHAPTER 6

The 19th Century

EUROPE

There is a pattern to the development of furniture design throughout Europe in the nineteenth century which, as each country comes under scrutiny, becomes familiar even though there are a few variations. It goes something like this, with the dates given as an indication rather than in any fixed rigidity:

1800-1820

The century opened with the French Empire style in full swing with dark mahogany severity of line and surface enlivened by exquisite gilded bronze mounts. In France, of course, this style was paramount until Napoleon fell in 1815, but shortage of mahogany due to the blockade led to lighter local woods – the *bois clairs* – being used. In territories which had been occupied by France – Belgium, Holland, Spain etc – the style was unquestioned. In England it formed the basis of the Regency style even though the 'Trafalgar' chair with sabre legs was held as a national design. In Germany it slowly gave way to the much lighter, simpler, Biedermeier version.

1820-1840

The Empire style, modified into a heavier sub-Classical style, died slowly away in favour of a confused historicism which amongst other things brought the 'Gothic' back to the fore although with little enthusiasm in Italy, where Gothic was never greatly favoured. Belgium took to this mock-Medievalism with fervour and kept it going to the end of the century. In England it was Pugin who led the Gothic charge but it did not last much beyond mid-century despite its strongly religious connotations. In France the style was called *Troubadour*, but did not do a lot of damage to the sub-Empire style still prevailing.

Apart from the Gothic, it was back to the Renaissance and the Baroque in Italy and France, with a Naturalistic style coming in which heralded the new Rococo. Eclecticism – picking from hither and yon – started to set in. Machine methods sped up production of the mass of furniture needed by a new European middle class whose taste had not been 'educated' like the aristocrat-patrons of yore.

1840 -1870

The Rococo style was in full flood in England, France and Italy. Many pieces looked much the same no matter which country they came from. The French of Louis XV gave way to Louis XVI and other combinations during the Second Empire. In Belgium 'Renaissance' and 'Baroque' pieces, as well as Gothic, were churned out to meet a fervour for the 'antique'. Even in Germany and Austria the Second Empire styles were widespread until, towards the end of the century, a reaction set in, spurred by England, France and Belgium.

1870-1900

Two major lines of development were followed:

The first was a 'tasteless' jumble of commercial production of spurious earlier styles or combinations, plus a substantial return to eighteenth century forms which led to outright reproductions of eighteenth century pieces. Classicism was back with a vengeance, even if not always very accurately.

The second was an Arts-and-Crafts, William Morris-style rejection of commercial methods in favour of the individual craftsman and conscious thought on modern design. The Art Nouveau style, whose sinuous curves deliberately avoided the limitations of the materials being used, was promoted by avant-garde and intellectual designers.

The century ended, therefore, with a welter of commercial and individual furniture production ranging from the cheapest mass-production, some of it terrible but not all of it by any means badly conceived, to extremely expensive craftsmanlike pieces made as faithful reproductions of earlier forms or in 'modern' designs which looked forward to the twentieth century.

1. An early 19th century Italian ebony and cedar console table with a black marble top. The style, called Etruscan, leans heavily on Classical forms, especially the use of sphinxes, and the back supports are the banded rods known as fasces, symbols of the power of the state to chastise (hence Fascism). The Egyptian analogy allied with the Classical tone reflects the prevailing French Empire taste in Europe.

2 (Left). An Italian simulated rosewood and parcel-gilt 'Klismos' armchair derived from the Greek but with straight front legs, using a fluted X-form back splat centred by a patera. The arm supports are carved with acanthus leaves and the tapering reeded legs are headed by paterae. c.1825.

3 (Above). An Italian giltwood X-frame stool of c.1800 with fluted arm supports and fluted legs faced by fleur-de-lis. Again a combination of a traditional form with French Empire influence.

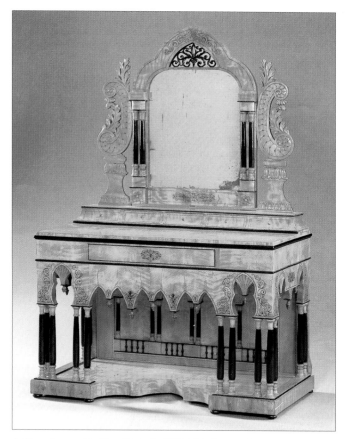

4. The reluctant Gothic of Italy in 1830. This fruitwood dressing table with ebonised columns exhibits more of the Islamic origins of the Gothic in both its arcading and decoration than the Northern French and English Gothic of more pointed and developed form.

ITALY

The start of the century saw French Empire influence at its height even though the restrained severity of the style was not very well suited to Italian temperament or skills. It was however popular for some time after the end of Napoleon's reign in 1815 and its distinguishing motifs of caryatids, Egyptian figures and sphinxes, and Classical paraphernalia appeared on much Italian furniture.

Italy was still divided into small states dominated by Austria in the North and was not unified until 1860. Many states continued to produce furniture in a traditional manner in regional styles that had been popular for many years: Classical in Rome, Baroque in Tuscany, painted Oriental exoticism in Venice, and so on. The Gothic Revival which affected both France and England in the 1820s and 1830s did

5. An Italian walnut and parcel-gilt centre table of c.1820, with pietra dura panel for a top, raised on three dolphin supports and a central baluster column, the whole thing sitting on a flat three-cusped base of a form found almost universally on furniture in Europe from 1820-1840.

6. An Italian scagliola and giltwood table of c.1830. The production of marble, pietra dura and scagliola table tops has been a major Italian furniture industry for many years, often aimed at an export market. In this case the base consists of a fluted baluster stem with dolphin supports and lion's paw feet.

7 (Above). The certosina inlay skills of Northern Italy did not die out in the 19th century. This Milanese cabinet of c.1870 is inlaid with ivory and veneered in ebony and uses a combination of decorative motifs which include female figures, foliage, berries, roses, grotesques, columns, cherubs, musical trophies, fabulous beasts, pilasters, further cherubs known as putti, and even geometric stringing.

8 (Opposite). The Venetian love of producing blackamoors also kept going strongly throughout the 19th century. This pair of c.1900, each holding a pole which could be used as a torchère, are fine examples of polychrome work and exhibit turbans and painted embroidered tunics. The simulated tortoiseshell and porphyry plinths are of later date.

not catch on very strongly in Italy – it didn't in the original Gothic period either (see Chapter 1) – nor did the Louis Revivals in their different manifestations. The Risorgimento of post-1815 saw an enthusiasm for the Renaissance in which Italy had played so central a part. A style called Dantesque, with 'Dante' X-stools upholstered in red plush and so on, culled from Renaissance designs, became popular. Later there was some English

9 (Top). Earlier Italian pieces were made either as reproductions or with the outright intention to deceive rich foreign visitors. This carved oak cassone in the Renaissance style, on hefty paw feet, would not perhaps be intended as a fake since it is so clearly of little age, but other reproductions were less easy to detect.

10 (Above). A 'Dante' chair of c.1880, showing the reproduction of a much earlier form (see Chapter 3) from the Renaissance, this time using inlaid bone and pewter geometric inlaid decoration.

influence in Neo-Classical Georgian pieces being made in Italy but this work, as with Italian versions of French commodes, was poorly made as far as the carcases were concerned. Round tables with mosaic or pietra dura tops were put on bases sometimes made in England and were aimed at an export market. One of the most influential factors in Italian furniture, from the Renaissance and the Baroque onwards, had been the use of sculpture and this continued to make itself felt. Blackamoors have long been an Italian speciality and these originally Venetian seventeenth century stands, candelabra or vase supports were made from that time to the present day. Indeed, it was in the nineteenth century that 'antique' pieces, particularly medieval *cassone* and so on, were made with the deliberate intent to deceive.

One of the shining examples of Italian originality, however, was the work of Carlo Bugatti (father of the French car maker) which, in the 1880s, was of Italo-Moorish style and then developed into an Art Nouveau design (called *gusto floreale* in Italian) when Bugatti moved to Paris at the turn of the century. In Italy itself a rather etiolated Art Nouveau style, partly taken from England and referred to as Le Stile Liberty, continued to be popular for a longer period than the Art Nouveau lasted elsewhere.

11. An ebonised brass and pewter-inlaid rosewood corner chair and a side chair by Carlo Bugatti of c.1900. Bugatti, an Italian who moved to Paris by the turn of the century, was celebrated for an Italo-Moorish style which he later abandoned for Art Nouveau.

FRANCE

At the start of the nineteenth century the Napoleonic Consulate (1799-1804) was moving into the powerful phase of the First Empire as we shall see below, but the furniture industry had suffered during the Revolution, particularly when the guilds were ordered to close down in 1791. A large amount of important furniture from royal and aristocratic chateaux had been purloined and sold abroad, ironically much of it to England, with whom France was at war. However, once Napoleon was securely on his Imperial throne he set about refurnishing many of the looted palaces in the very identifiable style known as French Empire.

A particular reference used for this period is that of Percier and Fontaine, who published their *Recueil de Décorations Intérieures* in 1801, a design book from which important pieces can be traced.

The First Empire (1804-1815)

The Neo-Classical basis of the Louis XV and Directoire-Consulate periods (see Chapter 5) was the prevailing style, with the sabre leg and those Greek, Egyptian and Roman motifs so dear to Napoleon I's heart well in evidence. All of Europe was clearly influenced by this style, emanating from so great a power which occupied many parts of the Continent, and its versions are also to be found in England, Italy, Germany and elsewhere.

The start of the Empire saw mahogany, used with magnificent bronze *doré* mounts, used almost universally. However, the English

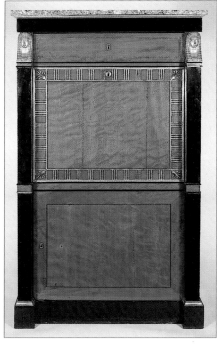

1. A pair of French Empire white-painted and parcel-gilt arm chairs (fauteuils) with scrolled padded backs and arm supports with tapering Sphinx heads. c.1810

2. A mahogany French Empire secrétaire à abattant (fall-front secretaire) again decorated with Sphinx heads in bronze doré in celebration of Napoleon's Egyptian campaigns. The cornice and pilasters are ebonised. c.1810

blockade affected mahogany in that it became very dear. Sources which were in the English colonies were effectively cut off. Cabinetmakers therefore turned to local and other European woods such as walnut, sycamore, ash, elm, maple and so on, with the now celebrated *bois clairs* – clear or light-coloured woods such as bird's eye maple – becoming fashionable.

The style was taken to severe, almost Spartan, simplicity compared with previous eras. Gradually, sabre legs were relegated to the back of the piece while the front legs straightened to turned, fluted, reeded or square tapering shape.

3. Two mahogany tables, known as guéridons, which illustrate common base designs of the French Empire period c.1815. The left-hand table, with grey marble top, has a solid triangular concave pyramidical base ending in lotus-scroll and paw feet. The right-hand table, also with a grey marble top, has a smooth column set on a three-cusped flat triangular base. This latter form is very common to many tables of the 1815 to 1840 period.

4. A low French mahogany commode chest of drawers of a type very common to the 1820 Restauration period and after. It has a marble top and the projecting top drawer is set above three lower drawers flanked by pillars capped with metal mounts.

The Restoration (1815-1848)
Louis XVIII (1815-1824)
Charles X (1824-1830)
Louis Philippe (1830-1848)

During this period there was a move towards more industrialised forms of manufacture. The ending of the guild system meant that Paris furniture makers could set up workshops combining all the required skills under one roof instead of separate specialised workshops for each trade. Their clientele had also changed in that there were many more of the new

5 (Left). A Charles X (1824-1830) mahogany extending dining table showing the ring-turned baluster-shaped legs associated with Charles X styles. Extending D-end (or demi-lune) tables of this type were also popular in England.

7 (Below). A French mahogany writing table of c.1820 which shows the traditional Empire features of smooth column supports capped with metal mounts still prevalent during the Restauration.

6. A Louis Philippe (1830-1848) rosewood X-stool with spirally-turned arm supports showing that the Renaissance X-form was popular not only in Italy. There is scroll and leaf carving which hints at a return to the Rococo.

middle class who wanted furniture and who did not demand the high standards of royal and aristocratic clients. There was, however, a great deal of political unrest, with Charles X abdicating in favour of the exiled Duc D'Orléans, Louis Philippe. Subsequently the 1848 upheavals brought Louis Napoleon to power and Louis Philippe was forced to flee to England. At this time many French cabinetmakers and skilled craftsmen also moved to London, where they continued their trade and produced furniture which is now very difficult to distinguish from French-made pieces.

The Empire style continued towards the 1830s but in a watered-down form with fewer bronze mounts. Inlays began to be used on many pieces and the austere outlines gave way to the greater comfort demanded by the bourgeois clientele who were beginning to dominate the market. As in England there was

8 (Above). Bamboo turning was not only an English Regency affectation. These French mahogany armchairs (fauteuils) of c.1825 are high quality examples by Jacob in which the 'sabre' front leg has been elegantly modified to take ring-turned 'bamboo' decoration.

9 (Right). The shortage of mahogany in France had led to local woods being used. Even after the end of the Napoleonic period, these 'bois clairs' – woods such as bird's eye maple and similar lighter-coloured woods – were popular. This is a Charles X console table of c.1825 with a white and grey marble top on bold cabriole scrolled legs which depart radically from 'Empire' columns and hint at the Rococo to come.

a reawakened interest in the 'Gothic', this time known in France as the *Troubadour* style, at first light and pretty, then heavy and medieval, and then the French Renaissance and a Naturalistic style also came to be popular, with all the eclecticism that also manifested itself in England and elsewhere during the century.

Boulle had also been revived during the Napoleonic period and it now flourished along with Louis XIV styles, which were popular for the dining room but which faded in fashion during the Second Empire.

10 (Left). The Gothic 'Troubadour' style in France gave rise to chairs such as this carved rosewood armchair of c.1840 with cusped arcading to the back and cluster-columned arm supports and legs.

11 (Above). By 1850 the desire to reproduce previous styles had become irresistible. This Napoleon III (or Second Empire) cabinet is ebonised, with pietra dura decoration to the central door panel and gilt bronze mounts. It shows no originality of design, using masks, acanthus, birds and flowers together with Bacchic masks. The glazed side doors are intended for the display of porcelain or similar wares. Such mid-19th century display pieces were also made in England, Italy and elsewhere, so that it is often difficult to distinguish the country of origin. In England they are misnamed credenzas by the antiques trade.

The Second Empire (1848-1870)

With the arrival of Louis Napoleon there was a return to Revivalism, for Henri II and Louis XIII of the French Renaissance, with Flemish solidity and gadrooned edging, eventually giving way to, or combining with, Louis XV Rococo and subsequently Louis XVI in various forms. Pastiche was all the rage – the

12. A 'Louis XV' giltwood console table of mid-19th century French Napoleon III period, with a Carrara marble top and a great deal of scroll decoration in addition to cabriole legs. The Rococo is well and truly back.

joke-term 'in the style of all the Louis' comes from this period – and Louis XIV was not as popular as his successors. Louis XVI seems to have become the favourite.

These revived styles, rather like the later Georgian Revival in England, were produced in multifarious forms, not always of the highest quality even though Paris still had the top *ébénistes*, until almost the end of the century. The new prosperous classes did not furnish in only one style; different styles were employed for different rooms and demand was therefore spread over a range of styles and combinations of them.

In 1870 the Franco-Prussian War had profound effects on the many German workmen resident in Paris and thousands of them returned to their native country, which benefited from this movement. It will become clear that with the moves described above – French to England in 1848 and Paris Germans back to Germany in 1870 – the seed for the International Style of

13. This French vitrine, or glazed display cabinet. of c.1880 is in the Louis XV manner, with cabriole legs and floral spray decoration. It is painted and lacquered in the Vernis Martin method first used in the 18th century (q.v.). There were many variants of this type of display cabinet, from single door to much more elaborate versions and the painted panels usually have Watteauesque scenes with gallant gentlemen paying court to ladies in this manner.

14 (Left). Boulle furniture was perennially popular in the 19th century and this French secretaire cabinet with arch-pedimented top of c.1870 shows all the features associated with the original inlaid metal and tortoiseshell decoration but used on a 19th century form. Boulle was also produced in other countries on similar pieces.

15 (Opposite). Combinations of sources were used in the 19th century. This French Boulle bureau plat in the Louis XV manner with cabriole legs mounted with caryatids, masks and flowers is 19th century carcase work using mounts and Boulle panels of 18th century origin.

16 (Opposite, below left). The Louis XVI style is said to have become the most popular in the late 19th century in France. This Japanese lacquer guéridon, or occasional table, could have been made then or at almost any time since. It illustrates the tapering fluted legs and spiky feet of the style under an oval top with a pierced brass gallery rail. There is a drawer in the frieze, which has four lacquer panels and the legs are joined by pierced interlaced stretchers.

17. (Opposite, below right) French historicism of c.1870-80. An armchair of 17th century style made of walnut, heavily embellished, in what would be called the Baroque Manner.

furniture was being planted.

The work of Louis Majorelle, a provincial furniture maker with large workshops who made all kinds of furniture but also used naturalistic forms of twisted leaves in broad mouldings, has been cited as one of the several influences which led to the more sinuous and fluid style which came to be called Art Nouveau.

18 (Left). Further historicism from France. A walnut cabinet-cum-dresser of c.1890 with glazed upper doors and much carved decoration including columns, acanthus leaves, cartouches, paterae, lozenges and all the language of the Renaissance.

19 (Below). Art Nouveau from France – an elegant table by Louis Majorelle, with crossbanded top, foliate frieze, and sweeping cabriole legs joined by an undertier.

20 (Opposite). A catalogue plate of Art Nouveau furniture sketched from the Paris Exhibition of 1900 by Timms & Webb. The sinuous curves and tulip whiplash decoration are characteristic.

The outstanding features of the style are whiplash forms, sinuous curves and broad, rather languid mouldings or stiles which eschew anything traditionally structural such as straight lines and verticals. It is as though the joiner is trying to deny the limitations of his basic material. The style was the subject of much comment and violent reaction from more traditional artists and designers.

Art Nouveau (1880-1910)

The origins of Art Nouveau are traceable to Gothic, Rococo and Japanese influences. In the main the style was a reaction to the Renaissance and Neo-Classical domination of the arts which had prevailed in the nineteenth century. The Symbolist, literary and artist-craftsman revolt against established taste which led to the champions of Art Nouveau declaiming their faith are too complex to be detailed here, but it can be said that the floral, naturalistic, scroll and languid, even weepy, plasticism of the style did not suddenly burst upon the scene from one detectable source. The term itself was coined by Samuel Bing, a Hamburg dealer who imported Japanese wares, mostly ceramics, into Paris, following the boom in interest in all things Japanese in the 1860s. His shop stocked furniture, paintings, glass and ceramics; he called the shop L'Art Nouveau.

1 (Above, left). A Spanish 19th century ladderback chair with ornate fretwork splats and matching front stretcher. Variants on this type of chair, including simple ladderbacks without fretted decoration, were made throughout the period.

2 (Above). The Spanish table remained faithful to earlier designs during the 19th century. This reproduction of the mid-century might easily have had iron scrolled supports below the top instead of the shaped longitudinal stretcher.

3 (Left). A sophisticated Spanish side cabinet in the Napoleon III (Second Empire) manner of c.1860 with marquetry and ornate decoration which includes gilt-bronze caryatids.

4. A Spanish cabinet on stand of c.1870 in the 17th century manner, inlaid with ivory and red tortoiseshell with scenes from Cervantes' Don Quixote. *The similarity to 17th century Spanish and Hispano-Flemish cabinets is marked.*

SPAIN

The distinguishing style of the first part of the nineteenth century in Spain was the so-called Fernandino, named after Ferdinand VII (1814-1833). It was a heavier form of French Empire incorporating gilt carved decoration, the French influence being very strong in view of the French domination of the Iberian peninsula until ejected by Spanish uprising and English help. There was also the influence of other prevailing European, particularly Italian, tastes which emphasised the importance of France. As with Italy, fashion trends briefly included the fleeting Gothic.

The Fernandino was replaced by the Isabellino when Isabella II (1833-1870) reigned and this was a more Baroque and florid style allied to French Second Empire, with much carved decoration.

After Isabellino came a return to sixteenth and seventeenth century forms, with the *vargueño* and the *papeleira* described in Chapter 3 coming back into fashion and being made in much the same way as before, so that these nineteenth century copies are hard to distinguish from the earlier models. The Churrigueresque style was also revived, bringing further Baroque extravagance and the classic tables with hooped iron supports which are a hallmark of Spain.

147

1. A mid-19th century Portuguese rosewood breakfront side cabinet embellished with much ripple moulding and flanked by spiral-twist columns. The four drawers are set above four mirrored doors. Mid-Victorian English cabinets adopted the same basic form but with different decoration.

2 (Left). A Portuguese rosewood side table, c.1865, of a design whose spiral-turned legs and stretchers are based on much earlier, 17th century inspiration. Again there is ripple moulded decoration to the top and the three drawers in the frieze have convex panels.

3 (Below). A Portuguese colonial rosewood brass-inlaid sofa of c.1825 of a form based on French Empire originals but somewhat compressed, with winged paw front feet whose proportion is too chubby for elegance.

PORTUGAL

In Portugal the Empire style, following the French occupation, was to be found every-where. There were, however, strong English influences which led to a Regency style of furniture and the German Biedermeier development was also popular.

The Spanish Isabellino style of the mid-19th century, allied to French Second Empire, was modified in Portugal to be less flamboyant, with more restrained carving. As before, Portugal used South American, particularly Brazilian, woods such as jacaranda and

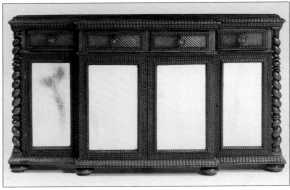

pausanto which allowed freer, crisper carving.

Many colonial pieces were imported, particularly from the Far East and Brazil.

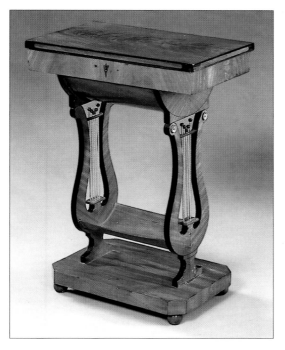

1. A Belgian mahogany work table of c.1820 in the French Restauration style. The lyre-shaped supports are joined by a dished stretcher and end in a flat rectangular plinth. The hinged rectangular top opens to reveal a well for the storage of work materials. Such work tables were very popular throughout Europe.

2. A carved oak serpentine front cupboard from Liège, second half of the 19th century, in an 18th century style. Carved pieces such as this, many of them in an eclectic medieval style, were a speciality of Belgian production in the 19th century.

THE LOW COUNTRIES

1. Belgium

Belgium became a separate country in 1831. The Empire style which had dominated the area gave way to Neo-Gothic with oak of medieval appearance and Puginesque forms providing a romantically antique atmosphere to many interiors. 'Gothic' cabinets of very loose interpretation were reproduced in large numbers. Indeed by the end of the century a form of English 'Jacobethan' furniture with much carving was made in such profusion in a style so similar to English carved reproductions that they are hard to differentiate.

There was a Rococo revival, as elsewhere, with Victorian Rococo chairs and similar pieces being made, but it was after the style had peaked in England, not taking a strong hold in Belgium until the 1870s. This Rococo also led to Louis XV revivalism and a lot of

3. A Flemish, probably Antwerp, oak stained pedestal sideboard of c.1870 in the 'medieval' style which Belgium produced so enthusiastically at the time. It is the equivalent of an English 'Chevy Chase' sideboard, plastered with carved game trophies of all kinds as well as caryatids and lion masks. In England such pieces generally were of mahogany or polished oak; they were not stained black in order to enhance the massive solemnity of atmosphere they produced.

ebonising went on.

Eventually Art Nouveau came to Belgium, with the work of Victor Horta (1891-1917), who designed a celebrated house in Brussels in the style, and one of its most notable exponents, Henry van der Velde (1863-1957), was also influential in Germany, having moved there in 1899.

2. Holland

At the opening of the century, in Holland as elsewhere, the French Empire style was dominant. It receded, however, in the face of

1. A Dutch semi-circular card table of c.1820 inlaid with floral marquetry. This type of tapering-legged late 18th/early 19th century opening table is to be found more in England and Holland than in, say, France. In this case the floral and vase motifs of the marquetry make it unmistakably Dutch.

2. Dutch marquetry tables, side and card, of 19th century date but using forms such as the cabriole legs which go back to the 18th century. In both cases the motifs include vases, birds, flowers and scrolls. The left-hand table has an undulating serpentine shape and is clearly a side table for occasional use. The right-hand table has a double-hinged folding top which can be opened for games use.

3. A Dutch mahogany clothes press of c.1800 with a canted, pierced fretwork cornice and panelled doors above three long graduated drawers. The fluted canting of the cornice is a feature of many of these Dutch pieces and the pierced cornices exhibit such variations as scrolls, balusters and fretwork.

4. Another example of Flemish medievalism, this from just after the turn of the century in 1907 but typical of such work, with Baroque 16th century devices including gadrooning, helmeted warriors, guilloche frieze, caryatids and recumbent lions, quite apart from the complex scenes carved on the door and lower back panels.

4. A 19th century Dutch colonial block-fronted bureau in a much earlier style (late 17th/early 18th century) made of a tropical hardwood. See Chapter 5 for details of oriental supplies to Western countries.

the Biedermeier style developed in Germany in which much lighter coloured woods were used. Germany and England still had a strong influence although French forms can be detected in much Dutch work.

The long tradition of marquetry decoration was still irresistible to the Dutch and later in the century they took to inlaying plain pieces of earlier periods, even inlaying Biedermeier furniture from time to time. The style of the marquetry was 17th century, with tulip flower-heads and baskets of flowers. 18th century designs of furniture were also treated to marquetry decoration with considerable enthusiasm.

Art Nouveau was not strong in Holland, the developments in this field coming closer to an English Arts and Crafts manner and to the latest styles of Munich and Vienna.

5. A Dutch ivory and marquetry table in the 17th century manner but made c.1860. The twist turning and X-stretcher are typical of the earlier type and these reproductions were clearly made to meet a demand for historical styles and fashions.

1. An Austrian walnut Biedermeier pedestal desk of c.1825 on which the Egyptian influence of the French Empire style still lingers in the chamfered corners with sphinx-like term figures of ebonised form and metal mounts.

GERMANY AND AUSTRIA

The French Empire style was the principal one used until approximately 1820 and Parisian craftsmen dominated many of the principal furnishing schemes. Empire was, however, the forerunner of the now celebrated Biedermeier style, in which the severity of the Empire furniture was relaxed to provide a more comfortable, middle-class and lighter version.

Biedermeier
The word Biedermeier itself was possibly coined after the appearance of the style around 1815 and is a composite word expressing a plain, ordinary man's taste. Comfort was

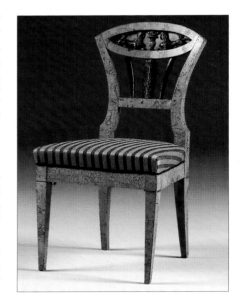

2. A burr elm ebonised and parcel gilt Biedermeier chair of c.1815 with ubiquitous sphinx figures set into the top rail above a pierced palmette splat. The square tapering legs emphasise the simplicity of this form.

3. Biedermeier sofas take French Empire forms such as sabre legs and simplify them to the point of modernity. This birch example with arched back and scrolled arms with ebonised rounded terminals is from c.1830.

4. A 19th century birch Biedermeier sofa of almost Art Deco appearance due to the fluted scroll supports to the arms and the scrolled sabre legs.

5. A Biedermeier sofa made of cherrywood, c.1825, with ebonised columns with metal capitals as front supports. Comfort was a hallmark of the Biedermeier style and many types of sofa were produced.

6. An early 19th century German mahogany secrétaire à abattant *(fall-front secretaire desk) in the 'Egyptian' style of the French Empire which includes a clock amongst its sophisticated decorative features. The panels of* pietra paesina *or stone mosaic work have been taken from an earlier cabinet.*

becoming more important than the severe elegance of the Empire. Biedermeier is noted for its seat furniture such as settees or sofas and armchairs of deep form. Round tables, chairs and china cabinets were made in large numbers as were all the variants of writing and work furniture: desks, writing tables, secretaires, cabinets, sewing and work tables are found in

7. A Biedermeier maple wood and ebonised secrétaire à abattant *(fall-front secretaire) of c.1825 with columns flanking the fall front, the interior central door and the door in the superstructure.*

8. A Biedermeier mahogany extending table of c.1820 shown in the unextended, circular state before extra leaves are added to provide the extension. The top has a brass moulded border and the base has four brass-bordered concave panels above a flat base with ebonised paw feet.

9. The 'Victorian Rococo' as applied to German furniture: a rosewood and gilt-metal mounted secretaire cabinet of mid-19th century date. Amongst the metal-mount decorations are masks, acorn finials and trailing floral and scroll work. The upper doors are banded and panelled in walnut, with marquetry figures of a dancing maiden and a trumpeting hunter.

this style. In North Germany the woods tended to be dark mahogany and the upholstery of black horsehair whereas in the South the woods were lighter, such as cherry and maple, whilst upholstery was not as dark either.

After the Biedermeier style there came, in common with the rest of Europe, a Gothic fashion followed by the now-familiar Rococo which was widespread in Vienna, where Louis XV was a style associated with greater days. This in turn led to the jumble of historical styles which set in elsewhere, with Louis XVI, Renaissance, Baroque and eclectic pieces being turned out in a variety of qualities.

Art Nouveau

The development of the Art Nouveau style in Germany and Austria came after its French and Belgian inceptions but had its first appearance in Austria perhaps as a development from Rococo. The work of Carl Leistler is celebrated for exhibits at the London Great Exhibition of 1851. It came to Germany later in the century, where the Belgian, Henri van de Velde, first exhibited in 1897, although there had been a German Arts and Crafts Exhibition in Munich in 1876. The work of English progressive designers was also influential.

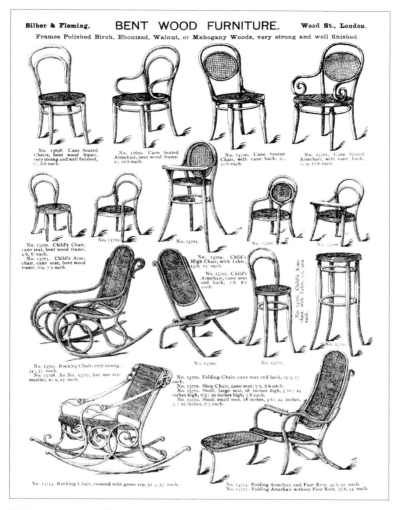

Silber & Fleming,   BENT WOOD FURNITURE.   Wood St., London.

Frames Polished Birch, Ebonized, Walnut, or Mahogany Woods, very strong and well finished.

10. *An advertisement for Thonet bentwood furniture from a London supplier. After 1850 Thonet's mass-production methods ensured a tremendous success and all kinds of furniture were made by the patent steaming process Thonet had developed. Some of the designs pointed the way forward to steel tubular furniture of the 20th century.*

Thonet – Bentwood Furniture

No mention of furniture in Austria in the nineteenth century could be complete without

Michael Thonet, who in the 1830s developed the bending of wood by steaming and the use of laminated wood to produce functional chairs

ENGLAND

1. Later Georgian (to 1811) and Regency (1811-1830)

At the start of the nineteenth century the prevailing style was that of Sheraton's later work, in which the Classicism which had come to England via France and the work of Adam was blended with the Egyptian motifs which Napoleon's campaign had stimulated. Later Georgian forms such as the kidney shape for table tops and pedestal desks, the rounded end as in sofa tables and some chests, serpentine fronts and so on were still in vogue. The Greek sabre leg chair derived from the *klismos* and a feature of the late Louis XVI-Directoire style

11. A bentwood Thonet armchair with a distinctive variant in the back design and a caned seat, c.1890. Chairs were also made with pressed plywood seats.

of memorable design. His curved, rather Rococo chairs were held together by glueing and were made of birch or beech. After 1850 mass-production ensured an enormous market for Thonet furniture, which now included tables, hat stands and a range of office and factory furniture quite apart from domestic and restaurant supplies. It was one of the first examples of mass-production on an unprecedented scale and millions of pieces were made. Later, the form and simplicity of Thonet's bentwood provided the example for tubular steel furniture of the twentieth century.

1. A Regency painted armchair of c.1805 showing the Grecian style with figures painted in Attic red. Note the slightly splayed front legs with ringed turning, hinting at the sabre shape and bamboo simulation. This Classical style is a result of French Empire influence.

2. An 'Egyptian' design from George Smith's book of 1808, in this case a painted and parcel-gilt armchair with lion head terminals, a Medusa mask flanked by scrolls, caned sides and lion monopodia front and back.

became the height of fashion despite its constructional shortcomings, but the form used was simple and the chairs light and elegant. In England, Egypt was rapidly associated with Nelson's victories, so that marine motifs such as dolphins and rope twists appeared as well as more exotic creatures and the lions which had long been great favourites. The so-called 'Trafalgar' chair, with sabre legs and rope or cable moulding was a typical example of this type. Simulated bamboo and more especially the ringed turning inspired by bamboo, which also came to England from France, was used extensively on straight-legged furniture. There was another Chinese craze, of which the Royal

Pavilion at Brighton was a particular example.

Two designers – Thomas Hope in 1807 and George Smith in 1808 – produced design books of great influence, in which Roman, Greek and Egyptian styles imposed on French Empire models were illustrated to the point of exaggeration. Sphinxes and chimerae (a fabulous monster with the head of a lion and the body of a goat, to which wings and serpents' tails were sometimes added) were used as supports and the mahogany surface of the furniture was embellished with ormolu mounts and motifs such as wreaths, honeysuckle, acanthus and others from the gamut of Classical decoration. The black inlaid

3. A Regency
mahogany bookcase
of c.1805 showing
Egyptian influence yet
again in the Sphinx-
headed canted corner
pilasters. It is inlaid
with ebony and brass
strips. Again a direct
result of Napoleon's
Empire taste.

4. A satinwood breakfast or dining table of c.1800 by George Bullock, with a rounded rectangular top
crossbanded in rosewood and hinged so that it can tip up – and hence be cleared away after breakfast. The
solid satinwood base has a sophisticated central pillar on four moulded legs with lion-paw feet clasping
ebonised balls. The tight scrolls at the top of the legs are an additionally crisp feature.

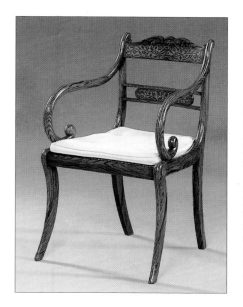

5. The sabre-legged chair was as popular in Regency England as it was in Empire France. This c.1810 rosewood chair is inlaid with a brass oak leaf and eagle design and has a caned seat with a separate cushion.

ebony stringing line was also used a good deal and the X-shaped stool reappeared, since the Classical provenance of the X-stool, one we have seen in earlier chapters, was so highly regarded.

Pedestal dining tables and circular 'loo' tables (named after a card game called lanterloo) or breakfast tables, also on pedestals, are a feature of this period. Brass inlays of floral and scroll patterns were set in rosewood as well as mahogany, sometimes to the extent of brass marquetry à la Boulle (see Chapter 4), but after 1820 satinwood and maple became popular in the style of the *bois clairs* of France. A famous cabinetmaker called George Bullock

6. The sofa table, intended for use beside a sofa, was a popular late Georgian and Regency piece. This partridgewood example has tulipwood crossbanding to the top and plain end supports with sabre legs joined by a ring-turned stretcher. c.1805

7. In England the term 'bergère' is used to describe a cane-sided chair of William IV and later origin, not the armchairs of 18th century France. These two mahogany examples demonstrate well-known William IV forms, the earlier chair to the right being of the squarer design while the left- hand chair exhibits scrolled arms and back rail.

was noted for marquetry expertise. Gradually, however, the lightness and exuberance of the curvaceous Regency designs moved towards a heavier form of Classicism now known as the William IV style.

2. William IV (1830-1837)

The Classical inspiration of Regency furniture gradually moved towards a rather ponderous appearance which fore-shadowed Early Victorian solidity. Chests and cabinets came to be mounted on plinths; the gadrooned edge moulding is characteristic; dark mahogany surfaces received less decorative treatment; hairy or paw feet peeped out from under pedestals; tapering reeded legs had pronounced reeds and even twisted reeds of more emphasised appearance than the slender Georgian versions.

Since it was a brief reign, the William IV

period has overlaps with Regency at one end and Victorian at the other, but the term is used to describe the heavier sub-Classical style which was, in fact, still prevalent for the first decade or so of Victoria's reign.

3. Victorian (1837-1901)

Until comparatively recently the Victorian period has been one regarded with horror by purists, who viewed anything made after the end of the Regency period as debased and decadent. The diversity and energy of the long Victorian period in Britain saw a growth in population and an increasing middle class demand which at first vehemently rejected anything considered to be 18th century in inspiration but by 1875 had gone back to the 18th century for its fashions. Since furniture was needed by new urban households which had little experience of acquiring sophisticated

8. The contrast between Regency-William IV design and Victorian Rococo is highlighted in this group of three incidental pieces. On the left is a William IV rosewood work table of c.1835 with a gadrooned edge to the top which lifts to give access to the silk work basket; below, it has a turned baluster support mounted on a quatrefoil (four-cusped) platform support on paw feet. The right-hand work box is Victorian Rococo, all curves and scrolls and cabriole legs, made c.1850 but otherwise intended for exactly the same purpose. Between them sits a Canterbury whatnot also in Rococo style. A Canterbury, a mobile piece intended for holding magazines and papers, is said to be named after an Archbishop of the see, and a whatnot is an incidental piece of shelved furniture.

9. The curvy Victorian Rococo button-back chair is almost a symbol of the period. Usually acquired as part of a set of nine pieces – chaise longue, arm (or gentleman's) chair, armless (or lady's) chair and six occasional balloon-back chairs, its favourite form is with cabriole legs and Rococo scrolls, plus carved floral decoration, as with this example of chair and chaise longue.

10. *The extending dining table was produced in large numbers in the 19th century. This rather aggressively cabriole-legged mahogany version of c.1860 has an undulating outline and carving which includes acanthus, husks and scroll feet ending in gadroons.*

pieces but which demanded something more fashionable than the vernacular country-craft tradition, there were great fluctuations in both styles and types. Machine production methods were developed rapidly and because much of this production was of cheap furniture for popular use, the application of the technology was both misunderstood and derided by those who felt they had a better grasp of aesthetic principles.

In brief, the Victorian period can be considered as having two major strands, viz:

1. General commercial furniture which followed a stylistic fashion starting with sub-Classical, going through Elizabethan/ Medieval, Victorian Rococo and so on until revived 'Adam' and 'Sheraton' reappeared.

2. The work of so-called Reformers and Architect-Designers like Pugin, Eastlake and members of the Arts and Crafts Movement whose influence was very varied and whose gospels were not always heard very distinctly.

This section will therefore deal with these two strands separately.

GENERAL COMMERCIAL FURNITURE

The Victorian period was fortunately one in which many design books and commercial catalogues of furniture were published. The movement in changes of styles is therefore quite well recorded.

Sub-Classical (1830-1850)

During the reign of William IV, the ponderous sub-Classical style associated with his name saw the use of pedimented furniture in 'Grecian' or 'Gothic' style, comprehensively illustrated in 1833 by J.C. Loudon's design book, take over from the lighter Regency fashion. With the accession of Victoria this style continued and much Early Victorian furniture is often wrongly classified as William IV.

The major characteristics of the style are set out in William IV above.

Elizabethan (1830-1890)

The Victorians were not very accurate in their

11. The Davenport is a small desk originating at the end of the 18th century. The name is attributed to the furniture firm of Gillow's, who made an early version for a client called Captain Davenport. This mid-Victorian burr walnut piano-top version exhibits the most desirable features in the later types: Fretted gallery to the pop-up top, activated by a spring mechanism and enclosing stationery compartments; bird's eye maple two-drawer interior under the curved 'piano' style desk lid; sliding ratchetted leather-covered writing surface; pen trough and inkwells; four short drawers set in the visible side and four false ones on the other; scrolled brackets, turned feet and castors.

terminology and what they called Elizabethan is not the pure Tudor-Gothic form we have described in Chapter 3. Victorian Elizabethan was eclectic and can be seen on pieces borrowing Restoration Stuart features such as the twist turning of the Baroque and the

12. The dressing table was an important bedroom piece. This walnut example of mid-Victorian date is a mixture of scrolled Rococo decoration and rather stylised column supports with floral carving. The oval mirror is supported on square section columns. The bowfront frieze drawer is flanked by short columns with downward finials.

cabriole legs of Louis XV. Sir Walter Scott's house was furnished in a variant of this style known as Scottish Baronial and the term Abbotsford is used to describe this mock-Tudor revival.

Victorian Rococo (1830-1890)

This is possibly the major style of the mid-Victorian period and is responsible for some of its most lighthearted and felicitous creations. It was a reaction to the ponderous sub-Classicism

13. The side display cabinet, now erroneously called a credenza, was produced in England in forms that were in many cases indistinguishable from French examples. This ormolu-mounted burr walnut cabinet of c.1865 has Sèvres-style porcelain plaques on the cupboard doors, each with a portrait of a lady. The projecting Corinthian columns have ormolu capitals and the ogee-curved side doors are glazed to reveal display shelves, usually velvet-covered.

14. This amboyna and marquetry card table in the 'Louis XV' style is of English make c.1860 but with its strapwork, foliate scrolls, cabriole legs and ormolu mounts it could easily be French. Possibly the work of expatriate French craftsmen in London.

15. The Windsor chair continued to prosper and was developed by industrial methods into many forms. This mid-19th century bow-back chair, whose turning identifies it as from the Nottinghamshire-Worksop, area is made of yew and elm. It has a complex scrolled pierced splat and a 'crinoline' curved stretcher between the legs.

of William IV and is characterised by the use of scrolls and acanthus leaf carving. The very decorative and plastic nature of the swerves and twirls it uses has made it a perennial favourite although by the 1880s its popularity must have died down considerably. When many people think of Victorian furniture, it is the Rococo they first imagine.

Georgian Revival (1865-1900)
A reaction to the curvilinear Rococo occurred in the 1860s, when Wright & Mansfield exhibited Neo-Classical 'Adam' style cabinets in Paris and London. Some people, clearly, had never abandoned a liking for the Classical and soon there was furniture with 'Adam' decoration in the form of inlays or painted decoration using swags and shells and floral motifs of Adam inspiration. This revival led to what has become called Edwardian Sheraton, a style current from 1880 to 1910.

The main thrust of the Georgian Revival, however, saw the return of Chippendale, Hepplewhite and Sheraton styles to popularity. Identical copies or mass-produced and weaker variants were made in large numbers and many excellent copies are now difficult to distinguish from the pieces of one hundred years or more earlier.

Edwardian Sheraton (1880-1910)
Strictly speaking this should not be in the 19th century chapter since Edward VII did not come to the throne until 1902, but in fact much furniture now termed Edwardian Sheraton and exhibiting all the characteristics of the style – satinwood as much as mahogany, profuse Classical decoration and inlays such as shells etc., etc., is in fact of Victorian date.

Victorian Queen Anne (1870-1900)
The term Queen Anne was used rather loosely by the Victorians, who developed an architectural style using broken pediments, dentillated mouldings, urns and fluted columns nearer to the William Kent of 1720-1730 than Queen Anne.

REFORMERS, AESTHETES AND ARCHITECT-DESIGNERS
Gothic (1840-1880)
Anything that carried a pointed arch was, to the Victorians, Gothic. Even Loudon in 1833 illustrated so-called Gothic pieces in which a gently-pointed panel was the only identifying feature. It was A.W.N. Pugin, however, whose ecclesiastical fervour for the Gothic led him to publish *Gothic Furniture* in 1835. This illustrated Gothic pieces of various types and led to the later Reformed Gothic of the 1860s favoured by architects who liked the idea of plain, joined construction in oak with revealed pegging and the celebrated William Morris-

16. A Gothic oak library table of c 1855 in which the work of Pugin has been influential in the essentially architectural structuring of the central column, which emulates stonework rather than wood. Pugin, however, used a simpler, stronger structural approach and the gargoyled carved decoration above the rather short feet would not have been to his liking.

17. The chiffonier is a side cabinet introduced in the 18th century as open shelves for books with a cupboard or drawers below. This c.1865 version with a davenport desk en suite is in satinwood and ebony in a style echoing French 'Louis XVI' taste. The open shelf has a pierced brass gallery and mirrored back, with ebonised mouldings and a spindled rail.

18. In the 1880s there was a Georgian revival, based on an 'Adam' style which led to Edwardian Sheraton in 1890-1910. This breakfront library bookcase of c.1880 shows the inlaid satinwood decoration associated with the style – swags, strapwork, paterae and even, in this case, Prince of Wales plumes.

type pieces which were painted and are now in museums. Other names in this style are Burges, Seddon, Webb, Talbert and Charles Eastlake, who published a book *Hints on Household Taste* in 1868 in which certain features – diagonal tongued planking, spindled galleries, inset panels and stained glass – were used extensively. Eastlake's book led to an Eastlake Style in America (q.v.).

Aesthetic Movement or Art Furniture (1865-1890)

Art Furniture, as it was called at the time, came about as a result of the Aesthetic Movement, a term generally describing a middle class enthusiasm for artistic matters as a reaction to crass commercial production. Most of this furniture is ebonised, i.e. black, with perhaps some decoration of painted or inlaid floral and

medieval-figurative form. A sub-section of this is Anglo-Japanese furniture and the work of E.W. Godwin who collaborated with a furniture producer called William Watt to produce a catalogue called *Art Furniture* in 1877.

The Arts and Crafts Movement (1880-1900)
Inspired by William Morris and Ruskin, a number of architects and craftsmen formed guilds and associations to produce individual designs removed from commercial furniture. These people and organisations included Mackmurdo, Baillie Scott, Gimson, the Barnsleys, Voysey, Ashbee and firms like Heals and Liberty's. They can only be related loosely to each other and there are overlaps with Art Nouveau.

19. The Aesthetic Movement of the 1870s resulted in much ebonised furniture with spindled turnings, coved tops, fielded panels to doors, bevelled mirrors and small glazed doors being produced. This sideboard exhibits most of the features involved. The only thing it lacks is for the panels to have painted medieval scenes in them.

20. Charles Locke Eastlake published his influential Hints on Household Taste *in 1868. It was an exposition of his ideas on the 'Gothic' style but he also illustrated works by other designers including the architect A.W. Blomfield (in whose office Thomas Hardy had worked) who contributed this oak cabinet. Eastlake furniture in America was a derivative of the published work.*

21. The English or Scottish version of Art Nouveau was not usually as sinuous as the Continental version. In this case c.1900 the essential structure of the piece remains faithful to its square construction but the decoration of inlaid floral forms, pierced scrolls and 'tulip' leaded glass is derived from Art Nouveau forms.

Art Nouveau (1880-1910)

A chair by Mackmurdo is often used as the start point for Art Nouveau in Britain but Charles Rennie Mackintosh and M.H. Baillie Scott are considered to be the local leaders of the Art Nouveau movement. The style is essentially French and the sinuous plastic style was not favoured by the doyens of the Arts and Crafts Movement. There is an overlap, however, between the two Movements and the

22. *The wheel came full circle with the production of 18th century styles from 1880 onwards. These Victorian Chippendale chairs with cabriole legs ending in ball and claw feet are not quite right by the originals but have considerable quality. Square-legged 'Chippendale' chairs were also much mass-produced.*

23. *The work of Charles Rennie Mackintosh is celebrated for its break from constructional constraints. Mackintosh was a highly influential designer whose work was much closer to Continental Art Nouveau than the Arts and Crafts work of English designers such as Voysey. This chair is one of his most famous designs intended for the Argyle Street Tea Rooms in 1897.*

more restrained rectilinear British Arts and Crafts style is sometimes confused with Art Nouveau because there are some motifs – pierced and solid heart shapes, and flat-capped uprights – which are common to both.

AMERICA

The development of furniture styles in America in the nineteenth century has some very close parallels with those in Europe and particularly England, although the new Republic understandably veered away from English styles for a limited period at the end of the eighteenth century.

The particular progression of historical influences on the mass of American furniture production has a familiar ring to it, viz.

At the start of the century, French Empire was the prevailing furniture for those intent on being *à la mode*. There were a number of furniture craftsmen such as Duncan Phyfe in Philadelphia who were already well established and who made furniture in the Empire style, although their execution increasingly meandered more towards the English derivative of French Empire known as

1. A Duncan Phyfe 'Empire' chair of c.1815 with sabre legs and eagle splat of patriotic motif. The reeded uprights and leaf carving mark the high quality of this chair, which is very similar to English 'Regency' chairs.

2. An 'Empire' solid bird's eye maple American chest of drawers or dresser with distinctive columns, cherrywood bandings and ebonised knobs, 1820-1830. The Empire style was the prevailing fashion of the first part of the 19th century.

3. An American veneered mahogany dressing table with spiral-turned legs and convex drawer fronts in the Empire style c.1820.

4. An American sofa of 1815-1825 in the Empire style with scrolled ends and sabre legs.

6. The Empire gave way to the Rococo, which was the prevailing style of the mid-century. This American sofa of c.1850 shows the scrolled, cabriole-legged and leaf-carved characteristics of the Rococo style.

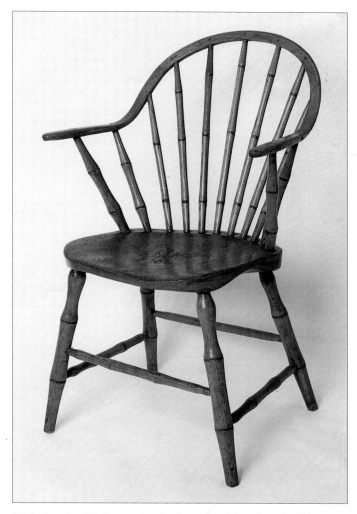

5. *The American Windsor continued to be produced throughout the 19th century. This sophisticated continuous-arm version of a type associated with New England, c.1815, shows the 'bamboo' turned decorative effects emphasised by yellow and black paint many such chairs exhibited as a result of European fashion.*

Regency. The Classical, Greek and Egyptian motifs of the Empire style were used by New York craftsmen such as the Frenchman Lannuier, Brauwers and others. Soon, however, it was the English George Smith's *Guide* which became the source of design ideas.

From the French Empire to a heavier, debased version, with John Hall of Baltimore's *Cabinet*

7. *The Rococo button-back armchair is a symbol of the mid-19th century period in America as much as it is for Victorian England. This has the pronounced scrolls, cabriole legs and leaf carving which are typical of the style.*

Maker's Assistant, published in 1840, setting the trend is but a familiar story. From this via a Gothic Revival to the Rococo is even more familiar to Europeans, and the Rococo, as in Victorian England, was the dominating style of the mid-century. In this connection the German, John Henry Belter of New York, became a leading exponent although he too moved on from the Rococo curves of Louis XV to the upright lines of Louis XVI as fashion progressed in America the way it did in Europe.

Other variations taken from the past, such as the Renaissance, were also used, some of this moving on into the form of heavier Louis XIV

8. An American walnut Gothic Revival bookcase with a faithful use of crockets, pierced cresting and the quatrefoil (four-leafed) arch to the glazed doors. The lower doors have blind quatrefoil panels. 1840-50.

9. *A commercial washstand in the 'Renaissance' style of 1850-1870, with pierced fretwork to the back and circular mouldings applied to give the effect of paterae.*

styles. It will come as no surprise to those who have studied the section on England in this century that the Louis XVI fashion was followed by a return to the eighteenth century of America's Georgian Colonial past with, at the end of the period, Oriental, Moorish and other eclectic styles. The commercial end of the furniture business had run dry of ideas and it required new methods and materials to progress from it.

Much of this nineteenth century furniture did not come from the fine craftsmen of the Phyfe, Lannuier and Belter type but, as increasing mechanisation took hold and mass-production methods spread, was of a cheap source with pine carcases being veneered in mahogany and walnut, with ornament merely a gesture in the direction of the so-called style

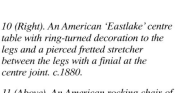

10 (Right). An American 'Eastlake' centre table with ring-turned decoration to the legs and a pierced fretted stretcher between the legs with a finial at the centre joint. c.1880.

11 (Above). An American rocking chair of c.1880 with ring-turned decoration stemming from Eastlake principles but Aesthetic/Japanese treatment of design and spaced turned framing.

12. This kind of American commercially-made dressing chest in elm and cherry is of a type made in birch and satin birch in huge numbers in the 1880s. The incised decoration lines come from Eastlake but the pediment marks a move towards the more architectural fashions of the end of the century.

proclaimed. One of the influences was Charles Locke Eastlake's *Hints on Household Taste*, published in England in 1868, which advo-

cated simple, honest construction and less decoration, although Eastlake was fond of inlays, bespindled galleries, diagonal planking,

13. *This American washstand in cherry and maple is of an early 19th century design which survived for a considerable time well on into the century. The rather elegant restraint of the turned legs, the shaping of the top gallery and the tray-shelf acting as a stretcher below are taken from late 18th and early 19th century 'Sheraton' styling which was predominant in England in the same period. The washstand was made by a Canadian craftsman, John Graham, of Ormstown, Province of Quebec, Canada.*

14. *Painted chairs were a particular American speciality of the first quarter of the 19th century. One of the most famous producers – and there were many – was Lambert Hitchcock of Connecticut who found a market in the South and shipped huge numbers of chairs from Barkhamsted, Connecticut, which eventually became known as Hitchcocksville. The chairs were painted by stencilling and virtually mass-production techniques were used.*

15. *The so-called Boston rocker of 1840 to 1890 was made in large numbers. The 'rolling' seat with curves at the front and back to provide extra comfort was especially popular. Shapes varied with fashion: in this case the vase-shaped central splat to the back and the broad top rail akin to the scroll back have both provided surfaces for painted decoration. The runners are extended much further at the back than at the front, which was found to give greater stability and was a feature of later rocking chairs.*

16. *A Shaker chair of the 19th century, with four slats and the arm posts terminating in mushroom-shaped hand finials for the front uprights. The Shaker sect, a branch of Quakers, formed in the 1760s in Manchester, England but having followers who emigrated to Upper New York State in the 1770s, produced furniture of admirable, if Spartan, simplicity in pine and local woods in communities in New England, Ohio and Kentucky in addition to their founding location. Tables, beds, chairs, benches and chests are now prized collectors' pieces for their functionalism and gracefully proportioned construction.*

incised grooving and architectural mouldings, not to mention stained glass panels. Much 'Eastlake' furniture in America is a remote derivative of the original conception, with almost any piece exhibiting incised decoration, spindle-turned galleries and ring-turned legs being described as 'Eastlake'.

During this entire period, however, there continued to be a strong production of American vernacular furniture by craftsmen not catering for city fashion. This vernacular furniture included the ubiquitous Windsor chair, the painted chairs of Sheraton style produced by those such as Hitchcock of Connecticut, and Shaker furniture, which was of admirably simple design and construction. The Boston Rocker is another American vernacular chair which was widely exported, as were many of these New England types.

Towards the end of the century American makers, including such craftsmen as Belter,

were experimenting with new methods of manufacture which included such techniques as laminating and steaming. The Thonet bentwood furniture of Austria was imported in large quantities and local copies were made despite Thonet's patents. Other methods and materials included papier-mâché, cast iron, wire and tubing. The scene was being set for a move towards genuine modern furniture design.

Selected Bibliography

General

World Furniture: an illustrated history – Edited by Helena Hayward. Hamlyn, 1965. Reprinted many times since.

The Journal of the Furniture History Society – published annually. c/o Victoria & Albert Museum, London.

The Dictionary of English Furniture by Ralph Edwards. 3 vols. Reprinted by Antique Collectors' Club.

Sotheby's Concise Encyclopedia of Furniture. Christopher Payne.

American Antique Furniture. Edgar G Miller. Reprinted by Dover Publications, New York.

The Art of the Cabinet. Monique Riccardi-Cubitt.

Early Furniture

Oak Furniture – The British Tradition by Victor Chinnery. Antique Collectors' Club.

18th Century

Pictorial Dictionary of British 18th Century Furniture Design. Elizabeth White. Antique Collectors' Club.

British Antique Furniture. Price Guide and Reasons for Values. John Andrews. Antique Collectors' Club.

18th Century English Furniture. The Norman Adams Collection. S. Whittington and C. Claxton Stevens. Antique Collectors' Club.

French Furniture Makers. The art of the ébéniste from Louis XIV to the Revolution. Alexandre Pradère

English Vernacular Furniture 1750-1900. Christopher Gilbert

The Oriental Influence

The Decorative Arts of The China Trade. Carl L. Crossman. Antique Collectors' Club

19th Century

Pictorial Dictionary of British 19th Century Furniture Design. Antique Collectors' Club

Victorian & Edwardian Furniture. Price Guide and Reasons for Values. John Andrews. Antique Collectors' Club.

Regency Furniture. Frances Collard. Antique Collectors' Club.

19th Century European Furniture. Christopher Payne. Antique Collectors' Club.

19th Century Decoration. Charlotte Gere. Weidenfeld & Nicolson.

The English Regional Chair. Bernard Cotton. Antique Collectors' Club.

Charles Rennie Mackintosh. Roger Billcliffe. Lutterworth Press.

Index

Page numbers in bold refer to illustrations